MW01146515

PEOPLE'S BIBLE COMMENTARY

NAHUM
HABAKKUK
ZEPHANIAH

JAMES J. WESTENDORF

PBC

CONCORDIA PUBLISHING HOUSE • SAINT LOUIS

Revised edition first printed in 2005.
Copyright © 2002 Concordia Publishing House
3558 S. Jefferson Ave., St. Louis, MO 63118-3968
1-800-325-3040 • www.cph.org

All rights reserved. No part of this publication may be reproduced, stored in a retrieval system, or transmitted, in any form or by any means, electronic, mechanical, photocopying, recording, or otherwise, without the prior written permission of Concordia Publishing House.

Commentary and pictures are reprinted from NAHUM/ HABAKKUK/ZEPHANIAH (The People's Bible Series), copyright © 2000 by Northwestern Publishing House. Used by permission.

Interior illustrations by Glenn Myers.

Unless otherwise stated, the Scripture quotations in this publication are taken from the HOLY BIBLE, NEW INTERNATIONAL VERSION®. NIV®. Copyright © 1973, 1978, 1984 by International Bible Society. Used by permission of Zondervan Publishing House. All rights reserved.

Manufactured in the United States of America

ISBN 0-7586-0437-8

1 2 3 4 5 6 7 8 9 10   15 14 13 12 11 10 09 08 07 06

CONTENTS

ILLUSTRATIONS

EDITOR'S PREFACE

The *People's Bible Commentary* is just what the name implies—a Bible and commentary for the people. It includes the complete text of the Holy Scriptures in the popular New International Version. The commentary following the Scripture sections contains personal applications as well as historical background and explanations of the text.

The authors of the *People's Bible Commentary* are men of scholarship and practical insight gained from years of experience in the teaching and preaching ministries. They have tried to avoid the technical jargon which limits so many commentary series to professional Bible scholars.

The most important feature of these books is that they are Christ-centered. Speaking of the Old Testament Scriptures, Jesus himself declared, "These are the Scriptures that testify about me" (John 5:39). Each volume of the *People's Bible Commentary* directs our attention to Jesus Christ. He is the center of the entire Bible. He is our only Savior.

We dedicate these volumes to the glory of God and to the good of his people.

The Publishers

INTRODUCTION TO NAHUM

Author

The only thing we know about the prophet who wrote this little book of three chapters is the information he gives us in the opening verse. His name is Nahum. Neither he nor anyone else with the same name is mentioned in any other place in the Bible. Other men like Naham (1 Chronicles 4:19), Nahamani (Nehemiah 7:7), and Nehemiah have names that are closely related to Nahum, however. So the name in its various forms may have been fairly common in ancient Israel.

Nahum means "comfort," and it's possible that the prophet may have received this name as a nickname to describe the message of comfort and assurance he delivered to God's people. It is more probable, however, that he received his name as an infant, well before the Lord spoke through him. Either way, the name is very fitting for this man of God. His brief revelation must have given much comfort to its first readers.

The prophet's home

There is much debate concerning the place from which the prophet came. Nahum identifies himself as an Elkoshite, an inhabitant of the city of Elkosh, but that's not very helpful because the location of that place is unknown. Three possibilities for its location are usually set forth: a site in Assyria (present-day northern Iraq), a site in Galilee, or a site in Judah.

The Assyrian location

Theories pointing to an Assyrian location for Elkosh should not surprise us. After all, almost the entire book of Nahum is addressed to the Assyrian city of Nineveh and speaks about events that take place in that area. Furthermore, there's a small modern village that has a name similar to Elkosh, Al-Qush. It's about 25 miles from the site of ancient Nineveh. There's even a tradition which locates the tomb of Nahum in that village. Anyone as familiar with the details of Nineveh as Nahum was—so the argument goes—would have to be from the area. His readers would then be the exiles that the Assyrian army deported to Assyria when it destroyed the Israelite city of Samaria in 722 B.C. This reasoning, however, is not convincing. The tradition that points to the Assyrian origin of the prophet is relatively recent, dating back only to the 16th century A.D. Furthermore, the book doesn't seem to be addressed to people who were living in exile in Assyria.

The Galilean location

In his *Prologue to the Prophet Nahum*, the fourth-century church father Jerome relates how a Jewish guide showed him a small village in Galilee by the name of Helkesei and claimed that it was the home of Nahum. Solely on the basis of this remark, some scholars advocate a Galilean location for Elkosh. It's easy to understand why the few Israelites still living in Galilee would be interested in Nahum's message. Assyria had long been the brutal oppressor of the inhabitants of that territory. Even before the kingdom of Israel had been overthrown by the Assyrians in 722 B.C., the great warrior-king of Assyria, Tiglath-Pileser III, had torn away the area of Galilee in 732 B.C. and made it into an Assyrian province. Already at that time, captives had been led away into exile. Now, a hundred years later, the relatives of those exiles who were still living in Galilee would be happy to hear about the impending fall of Nineveh.

Yet, there are reasons to doubt the Galilean location. At Nahum's time—a century after Galilee was added to the Assyrian Empire—most of the inhabitants were no longer Israelites. These new inhabitants had been forcibly settled in the area by Assyrian kings—in keeping with their foreign policy of uprooting native populations and supplanting them with people from other countries. So a prophet coming from this particular area at this time would have been most unlikely.

Other scholars identify Nahum's hometown with Capernaum, which means "village of Nahum." But as noted above, Nahum was probably a common name in Israel, and the village could have been named after any number of men with the same name.

The Judean location

No one location in the southern part of Canaan can be pointed to as the likely location of Elkosh, but a Judean location for the village has several things going for it. First of all, it's the most likely place for a prophet of Israel to be working in the seventh century B.C. The northern kingdom of Israel had already been destroyed. The southern kingdom of Judah was the only territory still left in the hands of the tribes of Jacob's sons out of all their original inheritance. Second, it is the Lord, whose temple was located in Jerusalem, the capital city of Judah, who was angry with the Assyrian king for plotting against him and victimizing his people. Judah never became a province of the Assyrians, but the little country had felt the wrath of this powerful empire and her mighty and cruel armies many times.

Finally, it is Judah whom the prophet calls upon to rejoice at the impending destruction of Nineveh (1:15). So the vast majority of scholars assume that Nahum was from Judah.

Date

Some Bible scholars argue that Nahum must have written his book shortly before the fall of Nineveh or perhaps even as the final battles were being fought in 612 B.C. To their way of thinking, the invasion of Assyria must have already begun and Nineveh was, perhaps, already under siege even as Nahum wrote. Such must have been the case, they argue, or Nahum could not have written with the certainty, the detail, and the vividness that he employed. Others argue that Nahum probably wrote only after Nineveh was destroyed and had lain in ruins for a number of years. They claim that it would have been humanly impossible for Nahum to look decades ahead and foresee what was going to happen to Nineveh. Such scholars refuse to believe that God can and did break through into the lives of the prophets to reveal the future to them. They assume that it's impossible, or at least extremely unlikely, that there is such a thing as true predictive biblical prophecy, where the Lord reveals the future to his prophets. They greet that idea with the same skepticism with which we greet psychics' prophecies about what is going to happen in the near future.

The Scriptures, however, inform us that the future is just as clear to the Lord as the present and the past. He knows the future because the future is in his hands, and he already knows what he's going to do in that future. In fact, the prophet Isaiah states that the ability to know and control the future is what separates the Lord, the true God, from all the false gods (chapter 41). Furthermore, God is able and willing to inspire his prophets to reveal what the future holds when it is necessary and beneficial for his people that he do so. So we do not have to tie Nahum's words to a time shortly before or after the fall of Nineveh. It is perfectly consistent with Scripture's testimony to place Nahum's prophecy well in advance of Nineveh's fall. In fact, that is part of their power and appeal.

So when did Nahum prophesy? The very earliest that he could have spoken is settled by his own words. He refers to the fall and looting of Thebes, the capital of Egypt at the time, as an accomplished fact. The Assyrians destroyed Thebes when they pushed their empire's boundaries to their greatest extent in 663 B.C. That was 51 years before the fall of Nineveh. If this event had not already taken place when Nahum wrote, his comparing Nineveh's fate to that of Thebes wouldn't have made much sense. Nahum therefore wrote his book after 663 B.C.

The latest possible date for Nahum's prophetic activity is not so clear, but there are a few clues. It would seem that when Nahum wrote, the king of Nineveh was still a powerful enough ruler to wield considerable authority. The prophet speaks of this king's continuing ability to "plot" against the Lord and his people (1:11). The last king of Assyria who would fit that description was Ashurbanipal, who died in 627 B.C.

Nahum also speaks of the yoke of bondage that rested upon God's people and refers to its removal as something that would take place in the future. Assyria's power crumbled after the death of Ashurbanipal. What little energy it had after his death, it spent keeping its enemies out of its homeland. It didn't have the ability anymore to try to control nations like Judah that had once been in its orbit of power but were some distance away from Assyria proper.

All these facts would place the time of Nahum's prophetic activity and the likely date for the composition of his book sometime in the latter part of Ashurbanipal's reign. A reasonable guess would be that Nahum wrote somewhere around 630 B.C. At that time the fall of Assyria was imminent—only 18 years away, but it would still take a prophet of the Lord to recognize that fact. During the reign of Ashurbanipal, a keen observer of the times might have noticed some cracks in Assyria's previously impregnable armor, but no one would have guessed how close the end actually was. The fall of Assyria and its capital, Nineveh, was as sudden and surprising to the people of that day as the collapse of the Berlin wall and breakup of the Soviet Union was to the people of the 20th century A.D.

Theme

Nahum's message is clear and unmistakable. Nineveh, the cruel, haughty, wicked, idolatrous capital of imperial Assyria, was going to be totally destroyed. Given the situation that existed in the Near East, that message was an incredible one, an almost unbelievable one. For years the Assyrians had been the dominant and most powerful nation in the whole region. Neighboring nations looked at them and assumed they were still savoring and celebrating their golden age—decade after decade of immense wealth and power.

More than once, the armies of Ashurbanipal had swept down the highways of Judah on their way to war with Egypt—the only nation able to stand up against the Assyrians and have at least a fighting chance to succeed. The Assyrian emperor, as was his custom, demanded that Judah, as a vassal of the king, provide troops for these military campaigns. He was quite willing for the blood of

Judah's sons to be spilled in order that he might realize his imperialistic ambitions. The tiny kingdom of Judah was powerless to resist any of these unwanted incursions. It had borne this yoke for over a hundred years, paying heavy tribute to the Assyrians all the time. And there seemed to be no end in sight.

The prophet, however, minces no words. He brings a message of judgment for the Assyrians, but also one of comfort and hope for God's people in Judah. It is only a matter of time—and a short time at that—before the Lord of history intervenes and Nineveh disappears—yes, literally disappears—from the face of the earth and her victims, like Judah, are set free.

Focused though Nahum's message is, it is still only a subpart of a much larger and grander theme. Nahum begins his book by describing the Lord—by explaining what the Lord God of heaven and earth is like. "The LORD is a jealous and avenging God," Nahum declares immediately after he introduces himself, "the LORD takes vengeance and is filled with wrath" (1:2). The Lord is good and loving to those who trust in him (1:7). This was not the case with the Assyrians who were arrogant and swollen with pride. The king of Assyria boasted about his military achievements in words like these recorded by the prophet Isaiah: "By the strength of my hand I have done this, and by my wisdom, because I have understanding" (10:13). Some 70 years earlier, one of Assyria's generals had stood before the walls of Jerusalem and boasted, "Has the god of any nation ever delivered his land from the hand of the king of Assyria? . . . How then can the LORD deliver Jerusalem from my hand?" (2 Kings 18:33,35).

Assyria was a sworn enemy of the Lord, and for that Assyria would have to face the Lord and his avenging justice. That would come in God's own good time. But when the Lord's avenging justice came, even great and powerful Assyria would not be able to escape or avoid it. The people of Judah were to understand that Assyria's fall and Nineveh's destruction would not *just happen* in the natural course of events. The Assyrian Empire, *the superpower of its day,* wouldn't just grow old and tired and go the way of all nations. No, the Lord God of history, who controls the destinies of all nations and all individuals, would bring about its downfall (1:8). The Lord would rescue his people from Assyria's clutches and remove the yoke of bondage from their shoulders. The Lord, as a just King and as the just and holy God, would carry this out.

Purpose

A discussion of the purpose of the book raises this question: to whom are Nahum's words addressed? With the exception of three verses in chapter 1 (12,13,15), the entire book is addressed to Nineveh or the king of Assyria. Yet it is doubtful whether the Lord ever intended for the Assyrians to hear Nahum's message. When the Lord did want them to hear what he was saying about them, he sent his prophet directly to Nineveh, as he did with the prophet Jonah (800–750 B.C.). So it would seem that Nahum's words were meant primarily for the people of Judah. The Lord, then, was speaking to Nineveh mainly for Judah's benefit. They were to "overhear" his condemnation. They were the ones to whom the good news of deliverance and the message of peace was directed (1:15). While they were merely bystanders—watching while the Lord carried out his just case against Nineveh—the few verses that do take them into consideration were there to remind them that God's justice was working on their behalf and for their good.

Nahum wrote his book, then, basically as a message of comfort and hope. Nations more powerful than the Lord's chosen people were always threatening their very existence. Assyria was one such nation, perhaps the most cruel and powerful of them all. The Lord allowed—yes, even had brought—the king of Assyria against Israel and Judah. Almost one hundred years earlier, he had said as much to Ahaz, king of Judah, through the prophet Isaiah: "The LORD will bring on you and on your people and on the house of your father a time unlike any since Ephraim broke away from Judah—he will bring the king of Assyria" (7:17). The Lord even spoke of the Assyrian army as "the rod of my anger" (10:5).

With these heathen forces, the Lord meant to discipline his erring people, not destroy them. And when the nation of Assyria had served the Lord's purpose, it would go the way of all the enemies of the Lord who arrogantly arrayed themselves against him. Assyria would be destroyed and pass into the pages of history. This truth makes the book of Nahum one of timeless comfort for the people of God.

Not many Christians begin their study of God's Word with the book of Nahum. And once they start scanning its chapters, they may be even more tempted to skip over the rest of the book, feeling that it has little to say to them. Such a judgment of the book of Nahum and its message is premature. For what Nahum gives us in his book is a specific, concrete example of how God operates in history, day by day, century after century—right down to the day and age in which we live. Yes, God is the God of history. He controls the destinies of all nations. Even the most powerful will be brought before him to give an account.

There have always been people who believe that they can resist the will of the Lord and destroy his people with impunity if they so desire. They despise the very idea of a just God who punishes those who violate his laws. They are badly mistaken! Nothing could be further from the truth! Jesus said that even the gates of hell will not overcome his church.

Assyria and her capital, Nineveh, were one ancient casualty of the avenging justice of God working on behalf of his people. The atheistic, communist government of the Soviet Union was a more recent one, and there will be more as long as this world stands. Nahum's message will never be irrelevant. It offers as much comfort to us as it did to Old Testament Judah.

Brief history of Assyria

To understand the full meaning and thrust of Nahum's prophecy, it is necessary to realize the dominant role played by Nineveh and Assyria in the prophet's day. The history of Assyria is intimately bound up with a territory known as the Fertile Crescent, which forms a semi-circle around the northern portion of the Arabian Desert. It is a narrow strip of cultivatable land between the desert to the south, the mountains to the north and east, and the sea to the west. It begins at the head of the Persian Gulf and runs northwest up the Tigris and Euphrates River valleys. (This would include the countries of Iraq and Kuwait today.) From there it swings west to the northeastern corner of the Mediterranean Sea and then runs south along that sea's eastern coast. The ancient land of Israel was located at the southwestern end of the crescent.

The homeland of the Assyrians was located in the northeastern portion of the crescent, roughly some seven hundred miles away from Israel and Judah. The upper portion of the Tigris River ran through the middle of Assyria, while mountains hemmed it in on the north and east. Assyrian armies often operated in those mountains and extended Assyrian authority into present-day eastern Turkey to the north and western Iran to the east.

For our study of the book of Nahum, however, we are more interested in the expansion of the empire to the southeast into Babylon and west to the Euphrates River and beyond. At the time Nahum wrote, the Assyrian Empire was at the height of its geographical expansion. It covered all of the Fertile Crescent and beyond. It included what today is western Iran, Iraq, Kuwait, eastern Turkey, Syria, Lebanon, Israel, Jordan, northern Saudi Arabia, and Egypt. A formidable, far-flung power indeed!

The history of the Assyrian Empire is a series of expansions along with occasional withdrawals and retreats. The driving force behind Assyria's expansion was twofold: the need for internal security (safe and secure borders) and the desire for international trade. Trade was the foundation of the nation's prosperity. Its favorable location on the northern reaches of the Tigris River gave the Assyrians the opportunity to pass goods along from Babylon in the southeast to Asia Minor and lower Europe in the northwest and from the east, sometimes the far east, to southwestern locations like Egypt.

In the earliest writings outside of the Bible, the Assyrians appear chiefly as traders. When they were powerful enough to do so, Assyrian rulers expanded their boundaries in order to protect their trade routes and prevent potential enemies from endangering their commerce or hindering their business transactions. When they lost some of their power, they withdrew to their original borders east of the northern Tigris River around their chief cities of Nineveh and Asshur.

In the later centuries of their history, the passions behind Assyrian expansion changed somewhat. Then it was their lust for wealth and the natural resources necessary to feed their luxurious lifestyles that fueled the continued expansion. Couple this with one of their religious doctrines, which held that Asshur—their chief god and the god of war—was destined to rule the nations, and you have powerful forces moving Assyria's expansionist foreign policy along. Assyrians felt that other nations should have no complaint—yes, even should be grateful—as the empire claimed its destiny and its armies overran their lands and took control of their possessions and their lives. Needless to say, this was not the case.

Assyrian history can be divided into three periods: the Early Empire, the Middle Empire, and the New Empire.

Early Empire (1813–1208 B.C.)

Although Haran, where Abraham lived around 2100 B.C., is less than two hundred miles from Nineveh, we hear nothing of Assyria at the time. The cities of Assyria, although important (Genesis 10:12), were just fortified settlements and trading centers on the Tigris. Much of the power in the area was in the hands of kings to the south, in Babylon and the surrounding area. Growing trade, however, changed that.

While Israel was in exile in Egypt, Assyria had its first known king. And less than a hundred years after the walls of Jericho fell, an Assyrian king crossed the Euphrates River heading west. The Israelites must have known about this growing power already at that time. For even before they entered the Promised Land—while they were stilled camped east of the Jordan—the heathen sorcerer Balaam prophesied about the eventual rise and decline of Assyrian power (Asshur) in Israel's territory (Numbers 24:21-24).

Middle Empire (1115–1077 B.C.)

During the time of Samson and Samuel, who served as judges in Israel, Assyria was experiencing a second period of expansion under its first king of note, a man named Tiglath-Pileser I. He boasted of crossing the Euphrates River 28 times and of reaching the Mediterranean Sea with his armies. The Bible makes no mention of Assyria during this period of Old Testament history, but Assyrian might and influence was drawing ever closer, now around four hundred miles away.

New Empire (934–612 B.C.)

About the time that King Solomon died and civil war split the nation of Israel into two kingdoms (the northern kingdom of Israel and the southern kingdom of Judah), Assyria began the period of its greatest power and final expansion. A series of powerful kings brought Assyrian armies across the Euphrates once again. This time they were not to be denied. It took only some 50 years for them to control territory north into modern Turkey and south into present-day Lebanon. The biblical writers remain quiet about the situation, although the writer of Psalm 83 does say that Israel's enemies were seeking Assyria as an ally (verse 8).

The first direct military contact between Assyria and Israel may have taken place in 853 B.C. Assyrian records tell us that the Assyrian king, Shalmaneser III (858–824 B.C.), fought a battle against a coalition of 12 kings who had banded together to defend their countries against him. One of the 12 may have been King Ahab of Israel. As a result, the Assyrians withdrew and left the area alone for a number of years. Only 12 years later, Jehu, the man who overthrew the house of Ahab in Israel, is portrayed in Assyrian records (on Shalmaneser's Black Obelisk) on his knees, being forced to pay tribute to the Assyrian king. (This is the only known visual of an Israelite king.) Again, the biblical writers do not give us this specific information.

The most significant and sustained contact between Assyria and Israel came in the final and climactic 125 years of Assyrian history. In 743 B.C., little more than one hundred years before Nahum was active, the most powerful and imperialistic of all Assyrian kings, Tiglath-Pileser III (745–727 B.C.), led his armies toward Israel and Judah. He invaded northern Israel and withdrew only when Menahem, Israel's king, paid him an enormous amount of tribute (2 Kings 15:19,20). At the time, Menahem headed the pro-Assyrian party in Israel, but there was an anti-Assyrian party as well. This party was headed by a man named Pekah. Pekah, having assassinated Menahem's son, eventually gained control of all Israel. Israel's new foreign policy was to form a coalition with the Arameans to the north in an effort to stop Assyrian expansion, as Ahab, it seems, had tried to do some one hundred years earlier.

Meanwhile, in the southern kingdom of Judah, another Assyrian vassal, Ahaz, was on the throne. He was so pro-Assyrian that Isaiah tried to warn him to act like a true son of David—to trust in the Lord and not to rely on great foreign powers. Pekah, for political reasons, also was concerned about Ahaz and his loyalty to Assyria. As a result, he tried to topple Ahaz from the throne. Against Isaiah's advice, Ahaz appealed to Tiglath-Pileser to help him against Pekah and Israel. The Assyrian king obliged. He was only too glad to interfere. He invaded Galilee and deported many of its people into exile, scattering them throughout the various parts of the far-flung Assyrian Empire. Then he tore the region of Galilee away from Israel and made it into an Assyrian province (2 Kings 15:29). This reduced the kingdom of Israel to a relatively small area around its capital, Samaria.

No doubt Tiglath-Pileser also encouraged an upstart by the name of Hoshea to rebel against Pekah and usurp the throne. In so doing, Hoshea became the last king of the Northern Kingdom. In Judah, meanwhile, Ahaz continued his pro-Assyrian ways, going so far as to replace the Lord's bronze altar in the courtyard of the temple with an altar dedicated to an Assyrian god, probably Asshur (2 Kings 16:15-18). For this Ahaz paid a heavy price. The Lord allowed an abundance of troubles to come upon him and upon Judah. It became a vassal state to Assyria—that is, it had to pay heavy taxes to the Assyrians for their protection. Ahaz himself had to go to Damascus and pay Tiglath-Pileser both homage and tribute.

As Assyria became more and more involved in Israel, Judah, and the surrounding countries, it came more and more into conflict with Egypt, farther to the southwest. Perhaps because she was closer to Israel and Israel's neighbors than Assyria was, Egypt succeeded in getting them to rebel against the rule of the Assyrians. For some reason—perhaps upon the death of Tiglath-Pileser—Hoshea, king of Israel, stopped paying tribute to Assyria and made a treaty with Egypt. This amounted to rebellion against Assyria. In retaliation for Israel's defection, Shalmaneser (727–722 B.C.)— Tiglath-Pileser's son and now Assyria's king—came and laid a siege around the walls of Israel's capital, Samaria (724 B.C.). He died before he could capture the city, but his successor, Sargon (722–705 B.C.), completed the job in 722 B.C. The Assyrians destroyed the city and deported the survivors into an exile from which they never returned. That put an end to the political existence of the ten tribes and of the Northern Kingdom of Israel.

Now only little Judah was left to face Assyria's might. About 20 years after the fall of Samaria, Sargon's death set off a chain reaction of rebellion throughout the Assyrian Empire. Hezekiah, the king of Judah—encouraged by the Egyptians—headed up a rebellion of neighboring states against Assyria's lordship. Hezekiah was hoping to reestablish Judah as an independent nation once more. So he refused to pay any more taxes to Assyria. This brought the new Assyrian king, Sargon's son Sennacherib (705–681 B.C.), to Judah. After defeating Judah's allies, he pushed back the Egyptian pharaoh, who had made a feeble attempt to help Judah out. Hezekiah offered to pay a heavy tribute to get rid of the attacking Assyrians, going so far as to strip the temple doors of their gold, but Sennacherib changed his mind and demanded complete surrender. Hezekiah refused. In 701 B.C. Sennacherib's army surrounded Jerusalem. All seemed lost. No one had ever held out against Assyrian siege machines for very long, as an Assyrian general boastfully and blasphemously reminded the men of Jerusalem (2 Kings 18:33-35).

But the Lord had other plans. Through Isaiah, he promised that he would not allow the Assyrians to enter the city—in fact, that not even one arrow shot by the Assyrians would land in the city (2 Kings 19:32). That night the Assyrian army suffered huge losses. The angel of the Lord passed through the camp and slew 185,000 soldiers. In the morning the ground was littered with dead bodies. The siege was lifted, and Sennacherib returned home. Sennacherib's own records say that his army left Jerusalem after receiving tribute and after shutting Hezekiah up within its walls like a bird in a cage. Those records do not say why Jerusalem was not captured. It was too much of an embarrassment for the proud Assyrian king to admit that he had failed.

This failure to destroy Jerusalem marks the end of Assyria's direct dealings with Judah. Like other small nations in the area, Judah continued to pay tribute to Assyria. But the kings of Assyria had their eyes on bigger game than Judah. They were looking to include Egypt in their empire. The Assyrian king Esarhaddon first attacked Egypt in 675 B.C. The conquest of the country was completed by Ashurbanipal in 663 B.C. with the destruction of the Egyptian capital of Thebes, an event that Nahum refers to (3:8-10). Egypt, however, was one thousand miles from Assyria. To control Egypt from that distance was impossible. Besides, Assyria was beginning to show signs of battle fatigue. The Lord's appointed time for its end was drawing near. By 651 B.C. Egypt had once again freed itself from Assyrian dominance.

With the death of Ashurbanipal in 627 B.C., the end of Assyrian power came quickly. Babylon gained its independence in 626 B.C. and even dared to attack Assyrian territory. The Medes, living in what today is Iran, began to push west. The result was a series of campaigns against the Assyrian homeland that climaxed with the siege and destruction of Nineveh by the Medes and Babylonians in 612 B.C. Assyria, with all its power and arrogance and military might, passed into the pages of history.

The city of Nineveh

It's not the entire Assyrian nation or even the king of Assyria that Nahum addresses most of the time. It's the city of Nineveh, the capital of Assyria, that occupies his attention. Nineveh was located on the east bank of the Tigris River. Its ruins, across the river from the modern Iraqi city of Mosul, consist chiefly of two tells (the Arabic term for a mound of layered ruins). The larger, northern tell is called Quyunjiq ("many sheep," a name that indicates how the site has reverted almost totally to a rural setting). The southern tell is named Nebi Yunus ("the prophet Jonah," so named by later Assyrian Christians because of Jonah's connection with the city). Separating the sections of the site is the River Khosr flowing west into the Tigris. Nineveh was named for the chief goddess of the Assyrian pantheon—known as Ishtar in Babylon.

In Nahum's day Nineveh was already an ancient city, around two thousand years old. In the Bible it's first mentioned in Genesis 10:11,12. There Moses states that the city was originally established by descendants of Noah's son, Ham. Ancient records in Babylon also refer to Nineveh's existence before 2000 B.C. Gradually, the settlement grew from a trading center and military outpost into a large metropolis. At its zenith the city itself was over three miles long and a mile and a half wide. Greater Nineveh—the city plus its suburbs—was about 30 miles long and 10 miles wide. One hundred twenty thousand people lived in the city. Many more lived in the surrounding villages. Together with the cities of Calah and Asshur, which were farther south on the Tigris, Nineveh formed the urban hub of Assyria. Most of the rest of Assyria was made up of peasants' fields.

Through all of Assyrian history, Nineveh was an important religious and political center. Before Assyria gained its independence and had its own king, foreign rulers had built temples there. And an Assyrian king who had lived some six hundred years before Nahum's day had built his palace there. Many kings who followed him did so as well, but for most of this time, Nineveh was not the Assyrian capital.

The city reached the peak of its glory during the reign of Sennacherib, the king who laid siege to Hezekiah's Jerusalem in 701 B.C. Sennacherib made Nineveh the capital of imperial Assyria. He rebuilt the wall around the inner city to a height of one hundred feet in places. It was broad enough to hold four chariots driven side by side. In the nearly eight miles of wall that extended around Nineveh, there were 15 major gates, each guarded by huge stone statues of bulls. Within the walls of the city, on the bank of the river Khosr, Sennacherib built a huge new palace. Around the palace were 9,880 square feet of sculptured stone walls depicting his many victories in battle.

The city was truly beautiful. Sennacherib himself saw to that. He laid many new streets and enlarged the city squares. He had a large botanical garden constructed near his palace and built a number of parks throughout the city. Sennacherib even built a zoo and populated it with exotic animals from his kingdom and beyond.

Such a great city with its sizable population needed a great deal of water. The most likely source, the Tigris River, was not fit for human consumption because of the heavy amount of silt that it carried. So the people of Nineveh had to turn to the much smaller river Khosr which flowed right through the city. Unfortunately, the natural flow of water in the Khosr was at its lowest ebb when the need for water in Nineveh was the greatest. In the hot and dry Assyrian summers the people and animals needed a lot of water. Sennacherib's many parks and gardens needed to be irrigated as well. Something had to be done if Nineveh was going to maintain both its size and its beauty.

Something spectacular is what Sennacherib did. He created a water system for Nineveh that was one of the engineering marvels of its time. To feed the Khosr and increase the amount of water available to the city, Sennacherib built 30-mile long channels from the streams up in the mountains down to the Khosr. At one place—in order to get water across a ravine—he constructed an aqueduct over 300 yards long and 24 yards wide. It contained half a million tons of rock. Then he dammed up the Khosr some distance above Nineveh to the east. That way the water behind the dams in the reservoir could be saved for the dry season, when it would be so desperately needed.

From Sargon, Sennacherib's father, to the last strong king, Ashurbanipal, Assyrian kings collected literary works, especially from Babylon, to the south. Old texts were gathered and recopied on clay tablets by Assyrian scribes. Then they were stored in stacks in a huge royal library. Archaeologists who have worked in Nineveh have estimated that over 10,000 separate texts are represented on the 16,000 clay tablets that have been recovered from that site. There is no evidence that the Assyrian kings themselves were literate or spent any time perusing their great collection, but they did the historians of our day a great favor. If they hadn't seen fit to collect these ancient works, most of the contents would have been lost for future generations.

The kings of Assyria lavished a great deal of wealth on Nineveh, especially after it became the capital city. Most of this wealth came from the tribute, or taxes, that conquered nations (like Israel) and vassal kingdoms (like Judah) were forced to pay annually. Furthermore, a tremendous number of slaves were necessary to carry out the ambitious engineering feats like Sennacherib's aqueduct. Those slaves also came from nations like Israel that had been conquered and led into exile by Assyria's armies. So when Nahum in his book described the city of Nineveh as "the city of blood, . . . full of plunder" (3:1), it was a very apt description.

In addition, the armies Assyria sent out in all directions came from more nations than just Assyria itself. Every Assyrian province and subject nation was expected to supply a certain number of soldiers each year to assist Assyria in her conquests. Soldiers of conquered nations fought under

Assyria's banner to conquer more nations, all to the glory of Assyria and her kings.

When the people from nations around Nineveh looked at the great city, they saw tremendous amounts of wealth— money and possessions that had once belonged to them. They saw magnificent buildings—buildings that had been constructed by their enslaved relatives. They saw the glory of the city itself—glory gained by the blood of their fallen sons and fathers and brothers. It's no wonder that Assyria and Nineveh were hated by those who had been crushed under its iron feet and forced to contribute so heavily to its greater glory. As Nahum prophesied, no tears would be shed when Nineveh was destroyed—unless those tears were tears of joy. Only smiling faces and clapping hands would greet Nineveh's downfall.

Assyrian military policy

When people who are familiar with ancient history think of Assyrian military policy, expressions like "excessively cruel" and "inhumane" almost immediately come to mind. There is good reason for that. The Assyrians committed one atrocity after another in the wars they waged. It was not unusual for them to maim their captives by pulling out the captives' teeth, cutting off their noses and ears, gouging out their eyes, cutting off their fingers and toes, or hacking off their arms and legs. Especially gruesome treatment was reserved for the leaders of the cities that rebelled against Assyria. Often they were impaled on stakes that had been set out around the captured city's walls. Or they might be skinned alive (done by experts brought along especially for this purpose, who could skin a person without causing him to lose consciousness—so that he could feel all the pain of having his skin peeled off). The skins of the flayed leaders would then be piled up at the city gate or hung on the walls for the horrified people to see.

The Assyrians' spin on this would be that they had good reasons for doing what they did. The purpose of such cruelties was to make an object lesson, or example, out of those who resisted the Assyrian onslaught or who rebelled against Assyrian overlords when the army was not in the area. In fact, we know about these atrocities only because the Assyrians themselves carved pictures of them into the stone walls of the long entrance into the king's palace in Nineveh. Any foreign ambassador who visited Nineveh would get a graphic reminder of Assyrian power as he viewed these scenes on his way to see the king. The reputation that Assyria had established by perpetrating such deeds no doubt made people tremble and led them to cave in to Assyrian might more readily. It also made people hate the Assyrians all the more.

The foreign policy of the Assyrians was to take many of the people they had conquered in their most recent war to their own land and settle them in Assyria itself or some other part of the empire. They then would turn around and replace the people of the land they had just emptied with people from yet another conquered territory. So when Assyria conquered Israel, many Israelites were deported as prisoners of war and then resettled in western Assyria and in Media far to the east—places from which these captives never returned. To resettle the abandoned Israelite cities, foreigners were brought into Israel. Later these foreigners came to be known as the Samaritans. The Assyrian general during Sennacherib's siege of Jerusalem told the men of the city that if they surrendered peacefully, they would not be killed but would be taken into exile. He also promised that the land to which they would be taken would be a land similar to their homeland, a land where they would enjoy good living.

The Assyrian officials in charge of foreign policy reasoned that displaced people living in a strange land would be less able to rebel against their rulers. The policy, however, built up great resentment against the Assyrians and made the time of Assyria's fall a time of great rejoicing throughout the territory of Assyria's domination.

Outline

The following outline will help to divide the book of Nahum into its component parts.

Theme: The Savior-God acts in defense of his people

   I. The title (1:1)

  II. A psalm of the Lord's vengeance and goodness (1:2-15)

    A. The divine truth—the Lord takes vengeance against his enemies and graciously delivers those who trust in him (1:2-7)

    B. The truth applied—Nineveh will be destroyed, and Israel will be restored (1:8-15)

 III. A prophecy of Nineveh's destruction (2:1–3:19)

    A. The destruction of the city (2:1-13)

    B. The cause of the city's fall (3:1-19)

PART ONE

The Title

(1:1)

1 An oracle concerning Nineveh. The book of the vision of Nahum the Elkoshite.

Before he begins his message, the prophet Nahum describes what he is about to say as an "oracle" and a "book of the vision." The Hebrew word translated as "oracle" really means "a lifting up" or "something that must be lifted up," therefore, a burden or a heavy load. The term then refers either to the voice of the prophet that is *lifted up* against Nineveh, or it is *the heavy load* of the Lord's judgment that Nahum is laying on the shoulders of the city. Whenever this term is used by the prophets of God, it usually signals that a pronouncement of judgment and doom is going to follow.

The prophet's words are directed against Nineveh, but Nahum's announcement of the Lord's judgment goes much farther than the city walls. Nineveh was the capital of imperial Assyria. Its splendor and power exemplified the glory and pride of all Assyria, the superpower of its day. So when Nahum addressed Nineveh, he spoke to everything and everyone associated with Assyrian might and glory.

It is unusual that Nahum's prophecy is also called a "vision." It seems like a double title at first, but it may be that Nahum felt that the first title was not totally adequate, that it didn't describe his message fully enough. As accurate as that term, "oracle," may have been to portray what Nahum had to say, the prophet wanted his readers to know even more about his words. The word "vision" has a different emphasis than the term "oracle." It speaks not so much about the *content* of the book, as it does about the *manner* in which God gave the message to his prophet. Visions, together with dreams, were ways in which the Lord had promised that he would reveal his Word to his chosen messengers (Numbers 12:6; Joel 2:28; Acts 2:17). Both Isaiah (1:1) and Obadiah (1:1) use the word as Nahum does, as a technical term for receiving a message from the Lord.

We don't know whether the *seeing* of the prophet was a literal use of his sense of sight or whether it involved God's communicating directly with the mind of the prophet, but the meaning is clear—this message is God's message. Nahum is not expressing his own opinion about what should or could happen to Nineveh. He is the Lord's mouthpiece—all that he's doing is conveying the words he has received directly from the Lord.

Nahum's message was totally unexpected. It came as a complete shock. After all, Nineveh was still in her glory years. That this tremendously powerful empire, this one and only superpower of its day, could fall—that was impossible to believe. Nineveh fall and be destroyed? No, that could never happen—at least not in the near future! Perhaps that's why Nahum put so much emphasis on the truth that it was the almighty Lord of the future and God of the nations who was revealing these truths through him. So while we don't know exactly why Nahum used this term, "vision," it does serve as a divine witness to the verbal inspiration of Nahum's message and assures us that we can look upon what he says as the Word of God.

Although other prophets have also called their messages "visions," Nahum is unique in calling his work a "book of his vision." This may simply refer to the fact that he wrote his words down so that they could be read, rather than delivering them orally and then preserving them in writing at a later time. The word "book" could also be understood as referring to a scroll. Then it would be emphasizing the fact that his prophecy was short and could easily be written and carried around on one scroll. Finally, the word could be taken in the sense of our English word *volume*. That would indicate that Nahum viewed his message as one of many the Lord had granted to his prophets and that it would form part of a larger work with a title something like "The Lord's Prophecies to His People."

Nahum gives his name and address in this title. No other source, biblical or otherwise, tells us anything about him. What an irony! God uses a humble, unknown man from an obscure village to speak his judgment against the mightiest empire of the day. Anyone who heard Nahum's words at the time he spoke them would more than likely have assumed that Assyria could easily afford to ignore Nahum's message, much as a charging bull can afford to ignore a mosquito. After 2,600 years, however, Nahum's words of judgment stand. Assyria and its capital, Nineveh, have lain in the dust for almost as long. The Lord may use the humblest of messengers or means to accomplish his will, but through them he can accomplish truly amazing things. That is true whether we are talking about an insignificant prophet announcing doom upon the greatest of world empires or whether we are speaking about the lowliest of women, and a virgin at that, bringing forth the Savior of the world.

PART TWO

A Psalm of the Lord's Vengeance and Goodness

(1:2-15)

The divine truth

The Lord takes vengeance against his enemies

> ² The LORD is a jealous and avenging God;
>   the LORD takes vengeance and is filled with wrath.
> The LORD takes vengeance on his foes
>   and maintains his wrath against his enemies.

Nahum does not proceed directly into the subject of Nineveh's destruction. He is a prophet of the Lord, and he wants the Lord's people to know why he is speaking as he does. Nineveh will certainly be destroyed—but the reason for that lies in *who God is* and how he acts in the world. So the prophet first explains what the Lord is like. He begins with a hymn describing some general characteristics of the Lord, characteristics that will come into play when the Lord begins to settle accounts with wicked Nineveh.

Who is this God that stands up to threaten great Nineveh, and why has he waited so long? Nahum introduces him as "the LORD." The NIV uses all capital letters to indicate that the word Nahum is using is not the normal Hebrew word for "lord" or "master." The word translated as "LORD" is the special, proper name that the Israelites used for their God. Some Bibles use the English equivalents for the Hebrew letters *Y(J), H, V(W), H* and then write the word in English as *Yahweh.* The Jews of post-exilic times considered this special name too sacred to speak or pronounce. So whenever they saw it written, they said *"Adonai,"* which is the normal Hebrew word for "master" or "lord."

Several hundred years after the time of Christ, Jewish scholars added vowels to the Hebrew Scriptures. (Up to that time Hebrew words had been written only in consonants.) When they did so, they put the vowels for Adonai under the consonants JHVH, to show how they wanted the word pronounced. If you pronounce the four Hebrew consonants of God's special name with the vowels for Adonai, you come up with the combination *Jehovah.* This has become a popular name for God among us, but it was never a name that the ancient Israelites or the later Jews used.

The word *JHVH* comes from the Hebrew verb "to be" and simply means "he is." That was the name by which the Israelites knew God, "HE IS." When God revealed himself to Moses at the burning bush, he used the name in the first person form and identified himself as "I AM WHO I AM" (Exodus 3:14). When the Israelites used this name, they thought of the God who had chosen them and had made a covenant to deal with them in his faithful love.

The name "HE IS" reminded God's people of his sovereign love. Unlike us, God is a being of independent existence and activity. We are and we act because God called us into being, because our parents passed on the gift of life to us, and because conditions on this earth are just right to sustain life. Without these we couldn't exist. God, however, is dependent on no one and nothing. He simply "is"—and he does what "is" wants. If he chose to love Israel and make them his own, the reason simply is because "HE IS," and he is love.

The name also recalled for Israel God's past faithfulness to his threats and his promises. Many times in the Old Testament we hear of the LORD, Israel's Savior-God, threatening to punish the wicked and the unfaithful and promising to bless those who cling to him in faith. He is the divine warrior, who destroys his enemies and rescues his people. He would often close his threats and promises with the phrase, "Then they will know that I am the LORD" (Ezekiel 25:11, for example). When the believers in Israel called God "the LORD," they were expressing their firm belief that he would keep the promises he had made to them in his love and that this same faithful love would also move him to deliver them from their enemies who hated them. Nahum assured his readers that God was about to act as the LORD. In love for them, he was about to move against their enemies. He is the God of free and faithful grace who will not allow anyone to trample on his grace.

Nahum's description of the Lord who was about to act was not a strange one that the Israelites had never heard before. He describes the Lord in the same way that the Lord had described himself. Read chapters 20 and 34 of Exodus, and you will find the Lord speaking of himself to Moses and the children of Israel at Mount Sinai in the same terms that Nahum uses here.

Nahum says that the Lord is a "jealous" God. When human beings are described as jealous, the word often carries an unsavory connotation, that of envy, jealousy, and suspicion. But when the Lord is called a "jealous" God, it carries no unfavorable connotation. It simply means that as man's Creator, Redeemer, and Sanctifier, he has the right to the exclusive devotion, obedience, and service of his people. It means that he will tolerate no rivals and that he can and does demand a fear, love, and trust from all mankind that flows from the bottom of their hearts. That is his right, and he will display his anger if that response to him and his love is not forthcoming.

In six other places in the Old Testament, God is described as jealous (Exodus 20:5; 34:14; Deuteronomy 4:23,24; 5:9; 6:14,15; Joshua 24:19). These passages include warnings to Israel about forsaking the one true God and giving the glory and praise that rightly belongs to him alone to the false gods of the nations around them. If they do that, they can expect to face an angry God, because the Lord is a jealous God.

Nahum's verse is unique in that the warning about the Lord's righteous and consuming jealousy is held before the eyes of a heathen nation. The Assyrians by their words and actions have challenged the Lord's ownership of Israel. Hence they can expect to face his jealousy in action. Perhaps the Lord held the people of Nineveh more accountable for knowing him because a century and a half earlier Jonah had preached the truth about him in the city of Nineveh itself. Whether that's the reason or not, the Lord wants his people to know that even heathen nations must acknowledge his lordship. If they don't—and especially if they willfully act against him and his people—they will have to face his anger.

The Lord's "vengeance" also plays a prominent role in Nahum's description. It is mentioned three times in this verse. Vengeance focuses on the Lord's retributive justice. God will repay all wickedness and oppression against his people, no matter how powerful and unstoppable those evil forces seem to be. What a sobering thought for believer and unbeliever alike to consider!

Nahum, however, is not finished painting his picture of the Lord's vengeance. We are to understand that he "maintains his wrath against his enemies." Human anger has a tendency to cool off with time. The collective anger of an entire community may flame against a person who has committed a particularly heinous crime, but after a while people tend to forget how angry they were. Their anger burns itself out. They lose their zeal to punish the wrong. That's not the way it is with the Lord. God's holy justice produces an anger that will not forget or disappear until his justice has been satisfied.

This truth is not to be confused with the human sin of holding a grudge. God's anger is perfectly righteous because it flows from a perfect justice reacting to human sin. Our anger at times may reflect God's zeal for holiness and can, therefore, be described as righteous and justified. But our anger is also tainted with sin. It displays a lack of patience and an unwillingness to forgive. Therefore, the apostle Paul quotes a psalm and says, "'In your anger do not sin': Do not let the sun go down while you are still angry" (Ephesians 4:26). Instead, he encourages us, "Get rid of all bitterness, rage and anger, brawling and slander, along with every form of malice. Be kind and compassionate to one another, forgiving each other, just as in Christ God forgave you" (verses 31,32).

There is one more thing that must be said about God's vengeance. It is his divine right to take vengeance, and his alone. He may at times delegate that right to certain human authorities, such as the government, but, otherwise, the Lord's people are not to take vengeance. Saint Paul writes, "Do not take revenge, my friends, but leave room for God's wrath, for it is written: 'It is mine to avenge; I will repay,' says the Lord" (Romans 12:19).

> ³ **The LORD is slow to anger and great in power;**
> **the LORD will not leave the guilty unpunished.**
> **His way is in the whirlwind and the storm,**
> **and clouds are the dust of his feet.**

It may seem strange to find the words "slow to anger" at the beginning of this verse. Nahum has been describing God's powerful, unstoppable vengeance. Why include a phrase here that is usually used in connection with the Lord's compassion and love? There are several reasons why this qualification of God's anger is necessary. First of all, the fact that the Lord does not get angry quickly might be misinterpreted as a sign of weakness or as a lack of commitment on his part. Nothing could be further from the truth. Divine justice is not weakened or set aside by apparent delays.

Being "slow to anger" is a manifestation of the Lord's patience. Through the prophet Ezekiel, the Lord says, "I take no pleasure in the death of anyone, declares the Sovereign LORD. Repent and live!" (18:32). The same patience that moved the Lord to send Jonah to call the Ninevites to repentance was now slowing down his terrible judgment. The fact that the Lord was "slow to anger" did not mean that the Lord did not have the power or the will to punish a haughty and hostile nation like Assyria. An unrepentant Assyria would eventually have to face God's wrath. God will not allow such defiance and hostility to go on indefinitely, as he assures us, "The Lord will not leave the guilty unpunished." Had it not been for God's being "slow to anger," the Assyrians would have been wiped off the earth long ago.

A second reason for the slowness of God's anger is his fairness. If the Lord punishes some nation or group or person, it is because they have brought it upon themselves. The Lord never punishes too quickly—before the wicked deserve to be punished, before they deserve to receive a full measure of the Lord's vengeance. This held true in the case of the Canaanites, whom we might be tempted to think were victims of God's love for Israel. God told Abraham that his descendants would have to wait until the fourth generation before they could possess the land of Canaan because "the sin of the Amorites has not yet reached its full measure" (Genesis 15:16). Then, before the children of Israel actually entered the Land of Promise, God informed them, "It is not because of your righteousness or your integrity that you are going in to take possession of their land; but on account of the wickedness of these nations, the LORD your God will drive them out before you" (Deuteronomy 9:5).

The Lord used the same principle in dealing with the people of Sodom and Gomorrah. Their wickedness was proverbial already in Abraham's time. But before the Lord made any move to destroy those wicked cities, he told Abraham, "The outcry against Sodom and Gomorrah is so great and their sin so grievous that I will go down and see if what they have done is as bad as the outcry that has reached me. If not, I will know" (Genesis 18:20,21). The people of Sodom and Gomorrah and the land of Canaan had not been victims of rash, unfair judgment from the Lord—and the Assyrians would not be, either. When these heathen nations earned God's punishment, he acted—and not one moment before. God is fair, but at the same time he will never ignore wickedness or leave the guilty unpunished.

As this verse closes, the Lord's way of dealing with the people he has created—and particularly those who resist him—is associated with the powerful elements of the whirlwind (or tornado), the storm, and the clouds. The heathen nations with whom the Israelites came into contact, including the Assyrians, credited these forces of nature to their storm gods. Nahum assures his readers that such forces rather are a manifestation of the Lord's power. The God who is the Creator and controller of such forces surely is a being to be reckoned with. His power and might and majesty must be feared and respected. By disregarding that power, the Assyrians put themselves in grave danger.

> **⁴ He rebukes the sea and dries it up;**
>   **he makes all the rivers run dry.**
> **Bashan and Carmel wither**
>   **and the blossoms of Lebanon fade.**
> **⁵ The mountains quake before him**
>   **and the hills melt away.**
> **The earth trembles at his presence,**
>   **the world and all who live in it.**
> **⁶ Who can withstand his indignation?**
>   **Who can endure his fierce anger?**
> **His wrath is poured out like fire;**
>   **the rocks are shattered before him.**

Psalm 106 speaks of the Lord rebuking the Red Sea at the beginning of the exodus from Egypt. It divided so that the Israelites could march through on dry land. The beginning of these verses may also refer to the exodus, but the scope certainly is not limited to that.

What the Lord has created, he can control or change. He can dry up any sea or any river, anywhere, at any time. The locations that Nahum mentions in and around the land of Israel—garden spots like "Bashan and Carmel" and snow-capped "Lebanon"—were known for their fertility and available sources of water. The abundant vegetation that such places produced, however, were still dependent upon the Lord's will. He could dry them up in a moment.

Nothing appears more permanent than the mountain ranges throughout the world, but the Lord can make them shake, level them with the ground, or even make them disappear. What Nahum is describing here is violent seismic activity. Whenever the foundations of the earth are shaken in an earthquake, people feel uneasy and powerless. Their sense of security and well-being is greatly disturbed. The Lord's power is in those awesome earthquakes, and he is greater than they are. Would it be any problem for such a God who spreads terror throughout nature to destroy Assyria? Would it be any problem for such a powerful God to destroy the entire world when his anger is aroused and he is determined to judge all wickedness? Jesus tells us that those same forces should remind us that this whole world stands under God's judgment and will be destroyed by the power of his word at the end of time (see Matthew 24:4-35).

Nahum now begins to make specific applications. What the Lord can do with rivers and mountains, he surely can do with individuals and nations. "Who can withstand his indignation? Who can endure his fierce anger?" Nahum's questions really need no answer. These are especially pertinent questions when that anger can be described in terms of volcanic activity, of fire that shatters rocks. If the Lord's approaching judgment is as irresistible as an advancing lava flow, not even the might of Assyria's armies would be able to hold it off. No empire since then, regardless of the power of its weapons or the size of its forces, has been any more successful than Assyria was when the Lord resolved to end its existence. With a series of very graphic descriptions, Nahum has painted a terrifying picture of the Lord's avenging justice and his supreme power. Nothing can stand against such a powerful and avenging God. If Assyria and its capital, Nineveh, is the Lord's target, then Assyria is doomed.

The Lord graciously delivers those who trust in him

> ⁷ **The LORD is good,**
> **a refuge in times of trouble.**
> **He cares for those who trust in him,**

Suddenly, the prophet's focus and tone changes. Nahum had been emphasizing the Lord's power and the way he displays that power in his acts of vengeance and anger against his enemies. Now he turns to a more comforting thought as he proclaims, "The LORD is good," and, "He cares for those who trust in him." The Lord has the good of his people at heart, and in "times of trouble" and difficulty, they will find that he is their "refuge."

In times of great danger, when an enemy army invaded, villagers in ancient countries would head for the walled city. Inside that city there would often be a second walled-in area: the citadel, or fortress. When the people entered that area, they were behind double walls, the greatest possible protection from the invading enemy forces. Nahum calls the Lord such a refuge or fortress. He offers his people the greatest possible protection they could ever hope to find.

Here is one of the many places in Scripture where the believer is assured that God is, indeed, a mighty fortress—that those who are his can always count on the Lord's goodness or faithfulness. Our faithful God will always have the believer's protection and deliverance as some of his top priorities. Individual believers, or the people of God as a whole, may well have to face forces even more powerful and hostile and deadly than Assyria. A purely rational assessment of the situation might lead to the conclusion that all has been lost, that God's people will perish, that God's purposes will be frustrated. Then trust in the Lord must push reason aside. Then the believer's heart must step in front of his mind and confidently declare, "The LORD is good, a refuge in times of trouble."

While his *focus* changed here in verse 7, Nahum did not change his *subject.* He still is describing the same God. Now, however, he is looking at the other side of the coin. When the Lord brings about the destruction of Nineveh, he will at the same time and with the same act be providing deliverance for his hard-pressed people. God's acts of punishment and vengeance that fall upon his enemies often mean salvation for his believers. Through the prophet Isaiah, the Lord declares, "The day of vengeance was in my heart, and the year of my redemption has come" (63:4). The Lord would provide the surest protection for his people by simply removing the threat of Assyrian power. That is why Nahum moves smoothly from speaking of the Lord's protecting goodness (verse 7) to prophesying the total destruction of Nineveh (verse 8).

The truth applied—Nineveh will be destroyed, and Israel will be restored

8   but with an overwhelming flood
   he will make an end of Nineveh;
      he will pursue his foes into darkness.

For the first time, Nahum stops describing the Lord's vengeance and goodness in general terms and speaks about the capture and destruction of Nineveh in very concrete and specific terms. Actually, the word "Nineveh" does not appear in the original text. The Hebrew text simply says, "But with an overwhelming flood he will make an end of its place." There is no antecedent in the sentence for the pronoun *it,* no word that *it* refers back to. But the context indicates that it's one of the Lord's enemies who will come to an end, and the enemy addressed in the title is Nineveh. So the translator's assumption that the pronoun here refers to Nineveh is a reasonable one.

There is no doubt that the imagery of an "overwhelming flood" is meant to picture some sort of a destructive force that will bring an end to Nineveh. In the book of Isaiah, the verb related to this noun is used to describe the hostile armies of Assyria pouring into Canaan and threatening Israel with annihilation: "The Lord is about to bring against them the mighty floodwaters of the River—the king of Assyria with all his pomp. It will overflow all its channels, run over all its banks and sweep on into Judah, swirling over it, passing through it and reaching up to the neck" (8:7,8). So it's possible that this expression used by Nahum is a figurative way of expressing how Assyria would be overwhelmed by some invading military force. Now Assyria's land would be the one flooded and destroyed by hostile invading armies.

In 2:6,8, however, Nahum points out the role that water would play in the Nineveh's capture and destruction. So the mention of the flood here is probably more than just imagery. It probably is a reference to one of the real-life agents involved in Nineveh's downfall—an actual flood. Nahum's point, however, is clear: there may be all sorts of natural and human forces which would play a role in destroying Nineveh, but the Lord was the primary agent involved. "*He* will make an end of Nineveh." God himself directed and actively participated in the events that turned this magnificent city into a pile of dust and rubble.

Nineveh's destination—as the result of the Lord's pursuing vengeance—would be "darkness." There is nothing pleasant about this description or about what it predicted as lying ahead for the wicked city. When God sent Jonah to Nineveh with the lamp of his Word and a call to repentance, Nineveh had been the object of God's grace. But now it would be confronted with the dark face of his anger. It's true that the population of Nineveh was enjoying the heights of its civilized brilliance and glory even as Nahum wrote. The people of Nineveh were the envy of all the other people of the world, but their future was going to change quickly! Soon they would have only the darkness of the grave and eternal destruction to look forward to. They and their enviable lifestyles would lie in ruins, and so would their wonderful city. God did indeed pursue them into "darkness." For roughly 2,400 years, Nineveh lay buried under huge sand dunes, undiscovered, unexplored, the very place of its once fabulous existence stamped "Unknown."

> ⁹ **Whatever they plot against the LORD**
> **he will bring to an end;**
> **trouble will not come a second time.**
> ¹⁰ **They will be entangled among thorns**
> **and drunk from their wine;**
> **they will be consumed like dry stubble.**

The footnote to verse 9 in the NIV gives a better understanding of what Nahum is saying. The prophet is addressing God's enemies. He is almost challenging them to oppose the great God of Israel. "Plot against him," Nahum declares, "and you can be sure that the Lord will foil your plans." That would be true even if at first it looked as though those plans were succeeding.

Assyria had plotted against the Lord and the land of Judah before. On one such occasion, Sennacherib, one of Assyria's great warrior-kings, invaded Judah. The year was 701 B.C., about two generations before Nahum wrote. The Assyrian armies seemed unstoppable. They marched through Judah and devastated many of its cities and smaller villages (2 Kings 18,19). Some of Nahum's older readers might even have been able to recall this terrifying event. But for them, the most memorable thing about that summer in 701 B.C. would not have been the might of the Assyrians or the havoc they wrecked or the huge amount of tribute they exacted from Hezekiah, but the failure of Sennacherib to capture Jerusalem.

The Lord changed Sennacherib's plans. He destroyed 185,000 Assyrian soldiers in a single night and sent Sennacherib home licking his wounds. No doubt the Assyrian king saw this as only a temporary setback for his plans. He would come back on another campaign and finish what he had started, but that chance never came. Other campaigns and other affairs of the empire kept him occupied for the next 20 years. Finally, he was killed in a palace revolt some 40 years before Nahum began his work.

So the Lord brought Sennacherib and his plot against God and the land of Judah to an end. No other Assyrian king after Sennacherib ever approached Jerusalem's walls with an army again. Soon Nineveh itself would lie in the dust. Then any and all chances to plot against the Lord would be at an end. Such a fate, we can rest assured, awaits all of the Lord's enemies, no matter how strong and glorious they might be. The Lord will put an end to them and their plans. Nahum now goes on to tell us how.

Only a very confused army would allow itself to become entangled in heavy, thorny undergrowth, making it an easy target for its opponents. Only a very careless or indifferent army would allow its soldiers to become drunk, thereby making them unfit for battle and incapable of defending themselves. Yet it is to these very depths—where they would find themselves helpless and defenseless—that the Lord would drag down the proud Assyrian military machine. Not only would Nineveh's enemies play a role in its destruction, its own fabled armies would self-destruct, leaving both the city and its inhabitants in a position where they could be easily destroyed like dry tinder or chaff.

Note the vivid contrast that Nahum paints. The inhabitants of Nineveh are dry, extremely flammable material. The slightest spark would set them ablaze. The Lord, on the other hand, is a flowing stream of fiery lava (1:6). Even solid rock, which does not burn, cannot hinder its progress or escape destruction. With such a contrast in the nature and power of the opposing sides, what chance would Nineveh have when confronted with God's fiery anger of judgment?

> ¹¹ **From you, O Nineveh, has one come forth**
> **who plots evil against the LORD**
> **and counsels wickedness.**

The fact that Nahum promises that the Assyrians would never be successful against Judah again did not stop the kings living in Nineveh from plotting against the Lord and his will for his people. Once again, Nahum simply uses the pronoun "you" in this verse as he used "it" in verse 8. The NIV translators' view of the verse moved them to insert "O Nineveh" for ease of understanding. We can agree with that insertion because there really can be no question that Nahum is addressing Nineveh.

The king in Nineveh at this time was Ashurbanipal, the last great king of Assyria. His greatest accomplishment was the conquest of Egypt, the only other nation at that time that could have been considered a worthy rival to his power. During this campaign the Assyrian armies were constantly marching through Judah on their way to Egypt. Assyrian records state that the king of Judah was one of a group of vassals who were forced to support this war against the Egyptians with money and soldiers. It might have been some resistance on Judah's part to help fund or participate in this military effort that caused the Assyrians to come to

Jerusalem and take Manasseh, king of Judah, captive to Assyria for a while (2 Chronicles 33:10-13).

> ¹²**This is what the LORD says:**
>
> **"Although they have allies and are numerous,**
> **they will be cut off and pass away.**
> **Although I have afflicted you, O Judah,**
> **I will afflict you no more.**
> ¹³ **Now I will break their yoke from your neck**
> **and tear your shackles away."**

Up to this point, Nahum has been describing the Lord's anger and goodness in his own Spirit-guided words. Now he quotes the Lord directly. Once again, just who is being addressed has to be understood from the context. As before, the NIV translators have added a name, this time "Judah," to assist with the understanding of the verse. Again, we agree with this addition. When the Lord says, "I will afflict you no more," he must be speaking to Judah. His message to Nineveh was the exact opposite.

The Lord acknowledges that, humanly speaking, Assyria and her armies were no small force. They were a formidable—indeed, seemingly invincible—power to contend with. And powerful as they were, they had many allies. Weaker nations are quick to curry the favor of a stronger one and often are more than willing to help it achieve its objectives. By doing so, they hope to avoid incurring the great nation's wrath and displeasure and, perhaps, even to share in the tribute exacted from the conquered nations and to share in its military glory. Countries that came into contact with Nineveh were no exception to this rule. Even before Assyria reached the zenith of its power, the writer of Psalm 83 said that Israel's enemies had sought out Assyria as an ally against Israel: "With one mind they plot together; they form an alliance against you—the tents of Edom and the Ishmaelites, of Moab and the Hagrites, Gebal, Ammon and Amalek, Philistia, with the people of Tyre. Even Assyria has joined them to lend strength to the descendants of Lot" (verses 5-7). In fact, Judah herself had engaged in this practice earlier. When King Ahaz was worried about an attack on his kingdom from Israel and Damascus, he disregarded the advice of the prophet Isaiah and sought the help of the Assyrian king (Isaiah 7).

Assyrian records show that many of the army units the Assyrians used in their campaigns were made up of non-Assyrian soldiers, soldiers supplied by Assyria's vassals. These nations were obligated by treaties they had signed—and in most cases were forced—to supply soldiers for Assyria's military campaigns. Other nations sought Assyria's favor and volunteered to join in their campaigns. These people were happy just to be on Assyria's side. After all, it was the side of a proven winner!

By contrast, Judah was in a pitiable condition. True, the nation still had not become an Assyrian province, as had Israel and its capital, Samaria. It still had its own king, and its people were all still living in their own land, but its situation was a humbling one, indeed. All that was left of Judah's territory was in the immediate vicinity of Jerusalem. The rest had been devastated by earlier invasions. Judean kings had to acknowledge their allegiance to Assyria and pay a heavy tribute each year, or face the consequences—something which Judah could ill afford to do. For any perceived act of disobedience on Judah's part, the Assyrian king would send his officials to Jerusalem and have them take hostages. No one in Judah had enough power to do anything about it. The Lord pictures Judah as being under Assyria's yoke as Assyria's prisoners and slaves, bound by shackles and chains.

The Lord reminds Judah that this Assyrian scourge in the land was not accidental or due to Assyria's unstoppable might. He had sent it. Assyria humbled and "afflicted" Israel and Judah because the Lord wanted them afflicted. The tyranny Assyria imposed was Judah's penalty for the disobedience and ingratitude they had shown to God. Already through Isaiah, the Lord had called Assyria "the rod of my anger, in whose hand is the club of my wrath . . . against a godless nation" (10:5,6). Of course, this was a stern warning to the faithless and impenitent people in Judah, who persisted in their wicked ways, but there was also a message of comfort here. If the Lord had willed to send Assyria, then he could also will to remove its presence once it had served its purpose. That is the Lord's reassuring message in these verses.

> [14] **The Lord has given a command concerning you, Nineveh:**
> **"You will have no descendants to bear your name.**
> **I will destroy the carved images and cast idols**
> **that are in the temple of your gods.**
> **I will prepare your grave,**
> **for you are vile."**

Once again Nahum abruptly changes the one to whom his words are addressed, and again our translation adds the name "Nineveh" in order to make the meaning clear. Nahum states that his pronouncement of doom upon Nineveh is not spoken by his own authority. "The Lord has given a command concerning Nineveh," and here are his very words.

In the previous verse, the Lord proclaimed freedom for his people. For them to possess that freedom meant that Nineveh would have to lose its power and control over them, that Nineveh would have to be defeated and destroyed. Now, the Assyrian Empire had gone through a series of reversals before in its history, but it had always managed to recover and come back stronger than ever. But this time, Nahum predicts, that would not be the case. This time Nineveh's ruins would not be rebuilt. This time there would not be enough descendants to even keep its name alive.

From the many inscriptions that have been discovered from this time in history, we learn that people placed the safekeeping of their memory and their reputation in the hands of their gods. The ancient Assyrians had a tremendous desire to have the names of their families and the record of all their conquests and achievements live on in history. They attempted to preserve them by inscribing them on the buildings, temples, statues, and monuments that they built. But now there would be no king, no place for the people to store the remembrance of their glory. Their gods and their temples would be totally obliterated.

Assyrian kings and generals had enjoyed destroying the cities and temples of the gods of the nations they had conquered. Now their own mighty gods would suffer the same humiliating defeat. Ishtar's temple in Nineveh was almost 1,500 years old. The city was named for her and was considered to be under her protection. Ashurbanipal had this invocation inscribed on a slab there: "For all time, O Ishtar, look upon [the temple] with favor." Now Ishtar would be shown to be a figment of men's imagination, represented by worthless images made of wood and metal. What a disgrace for haughty Nineveh and her arrogant rulers!

> [15] **Look, there on the mountains,**
> **the feet of one who brings good news,**
> **who proclaims peace!**
> **Celebrate your festivals, O Judah,**
> **and fulfill your vows.**
> **No more will the wicked invade you;**
> **they will be completely destroyed.**

Nahum now paints the picture of a military courier racing back from the battlefront on his way to deliver good news to the king of Judah and his people. The battle is won. Judah is finally free. What a beautiful scene these words must have painted for the people of Judah! There on the highest mountain in Judah stands a messenger calling out at the top of his voice, "Have no fear! Nineveh is destroyed! God's people are safe!"

The image of a messenger proclaiming God's deliverance from a mountaintop is not original with Nahum. Some eight years earlier, Isaiah had said, "How beautiful on the mountains are the feet of those who bring good news, who proclaim peace, who bring good tidings, who proclaim salvation, who say to Zion, 'Your God reigns!'" (52:7). Although Isaiah's message was written down some 80 years before Nahum was active, it was directed to the people from Judah who would be living a generation after Nahum's time. Those people would be spending their lives in exile in Babylon. Isaiah's words were intended to assure these people that they would experience the Lord's deliverance as he led them back from captivity to their homeland.

But Isaiah's words speak of more than earthly rescue. Isaiah brought great comfort to his audience with his proclamation that one day the Lord would announce a far greater deliverance from sin and death through his chosen Messiah. In Romans, Saint Paul quoted Isaiah's words to this effect and applied the activity to preachers of the gospel:

> As the Scripture says, . . . "Everyone who calls on the name of the Lord will be saved."
>
> How, then, can they call on the one they have not believed in? And how can they believe in the one of whom they have not heard? And how can they hear without

> someone preaching to them? And how can
> they preach unless they are sent? As it is
> written, "How beautiful are the feet of those
> who bring good news!" (10:11-15)

How fitting that Nahum should find use for this image as well! Whenever messengers come to God's people announcing that he has delivered them, it is always a time of the greatest beauty and peace.

Even though Assyria has not yet been conquered, Nahum speaks of its fall as an accomplished fact. Even now he assures the people of Judah that their sufferings are over, that they are free from the tyrant's yoke. He calls upon them to celebrate their festivals and fulfill the vows they had made in the Lord's name. This call is first of all a call to freedom. Under the Assyrian "yoke" (1:13), Judah often did not have the freedom to worship as the Lord had directed. At times the Assyrians even demanded that the people of Judah worship their gods. King Ahaz, for example, even replaced the large bronze altar for offering sacrifices to the Lord in the temple courtyard with an altar dedicated to an Assyrian god, probably Asshur (2 Kings 16:10-18).

One of the chief ways that we proclaim and give thanks for the gift of freedom we have here in the United States is by worshiping not according to some governmental edict, but as the Lord our God has directed us. Judah's return to her divinely directed worship and devotion to the Lord would make the same proclamation, "We are free from the enslavement of men."

There was another aspect to Nahum's call for celebration. As is the case with our major Christian festivals of Christmas, Easter, and Pentecost, Israel's festivals celebrated blessings, often in the form of deliverance, that the Lord had given his people. The Passover, observed in early spring at the time of the barley harvest, commemorated how the Lord had brought his people out of bondage in Egypt. The Festival of Weeks, observed in late spring at the time of the wheat harvest, called to mind how richly Israel had been blessed with crops and other forms of daily bread in the Promised Land. Later it also reminded Israel of the law that the Lord had given to the nation at Sinai through Moses. The third chief celebration, the Festival of Booths, was observed in early fall at the time of the grape harvest. This festival provided an opportunity for the Israelites to remember the way that the Lord had protected and provided for them when they lived in tents, or booths, out in the wilderness before he faithfully brought them into the land of Canaan under Joshua. Each of these festivals had an aspect of thanksgiving for the ripening and harvesting of a seasonal crop connected with it. More important, however, the Lord had attached the significance of deliverance and spiritual blessing to these observances. Now, once again, the observance of these festivals by Nahum's original readers would vividly remind them that their faithful God had been true to his word. He had delivered them, just as he had promised.

PART THREE

A Prophecy of Nineveh's Destruction
(2:1–3:19)

The destruction of the city

2 An attacker advances against you, Nineveh.
Guard the fortress,
watch the road,
brace yourselves,
marshal all your strength!

² The LORD will restore the splendor of Jacob
like the splendor of Israel,
though destroyers have laid them waste
and have ruined their vines.

Up to now, Nahum has been painting God's vengeance on Nineveh in mostly general, broad strokes. Now he tells us more in detail about the attack on the Assyrian capital and its defeat and destruction.

As Nahum wrote, the Assyrian king Ashurbanipal still sat securely on his throne in Nineveh, but Nahum's prophecy looks into the future. He sees the enemy armies that would bring about Nineveh's destruction and pictures them as already advancing through Nineveh's suburbs and getting ready to attack the city itself. It is as though Nahum has been transported some 25 or 30 years into the future, to the year 612 B.C. From that prophetic viewpoint, he describes what he sees: the army of the Medes and Babylonians racing into the metropolitan area of Nineveh.

How amazed, perhaps even incredulous, the people of Nahum's day would have been as they read what Nahum had to say about this incredible turn of events. What thoughts must have raced through their minds: "How is it possible for such a mighty city to fall in this way? How can these words ever come true?" How much more amazed they must have been several decades later when everything happened just as the Lord had revealed it to Nahum.

"Prepare for war! The enemy is approaching! You can already see the dust rising in the distance as they march down the road!" So Nahum cries out in prophecy to the doomed city, raising the alarm, calling on them to defend themselves and protect the roads leading to the city as best they could. There would have been thousands of people living in villages, on farms, and along the many roads leading to Nineveh—perhaps even hundreds of thousands. Some of them were the farmers who raised crops in the area. Others worked in the city but lived in the nearby suburbs. Still others were the merchants who sold food and water and goods to the large number of travelers who came to Nineveh every day. Their shops and stalls and stores and carts lined the roads and occupied the intersections, much like our malls and strip malls and supermarkets and individual stores and farmers' markets fill the suburbs around our large cities today.

All these people lived outside the huge central city walls. They would have been among the first to hear about and react to the news that enemy armies were marching toward them. Some would leave their homes and fields or places of business and seek refuge behind the thick walls of the city itself. Others would flee into the countryside. Still others would stay where they were, hoping that the Assyrian forces which had always been able to protect them in the past would be able to do so now.

There may have been some doubt in their minds, however. Military campaigns had always been frequent in Assyria's history. The armies of the empire always seemed to be fighting against some enemy or other. Up to now, however, these battles had always occurred far, far away in other people's countries, and Assyria had always won them. No foreign army in recent memory had even dared to enter Assyria. In fact, such an invasion simply could never happen in their lifetime—or so they had believed.

But now things were different. Assyrian cities just a few miles down the Tigris River—cities like Asshur, the old capital and religious center of the empire—had been captured and plundered by this same enemy just two years earlier, in 614 B.C., and those enemy forces were now closing in on Nineveh itself. Could they be stopped? No doubt the government would try. Every soldier stationed in and around Nineveh would be pressed into action. Divisions would be brought in from the far reaches of the empire. The most valiant attempt possible would be made to defend the city. But the very fact that the armies of the empire had been unable to prevent its enemies from approaching metropolitan Nineveh must have filled people's minds with fear and dread.

Nahum's call into the future allows us to imagine the doubts and fears that must have filled the minds of the Assyrian soldiers who were being called upon to defend the roads leading into the city. Younger recruits would recall the stories of great Assyrian victories that the veteran soldiers had told to entertain and inspire them. Nothing had stopped the Assyrian army in those days. Even if these veterans had exaggerated somewhat as they related their war stories, their accounts weren't far from the truth. Victory was always a foregone conclusion when they went into battle. Every campaign meant glory and riches for Nineveh.

Recently, however, things had not gone well. The past three or four years had seen the territory of Assyria shrink in size. Victories had been few and far between. Men who just a few years before had been vassals of Assyria—men like the king of the Medes and Nabopolassar, king of the Babylonians—had now become daring enough to threaten the very existence of their Assyrian overlords. So it was with anxiety and foreboding that the soldiers took up their positions to defend the roads leading to Nineveh. The situation didn't look good. Never had they experienced such desperate circumstances before.

How often Nahum's words "Guard the fortress, watch the road, brace yourselves, marshal all your strength" must have echoed through the hills and valleys of the countries conquered by the Assyrians in the past. In vain had the kings of other lands closed the gates of their cities and fortified their walls against the army of the king who sat enthroned in Nineveh, but to no avail. Now the tables would be turned. Now it would be Nineveh who hastily mustered its soldiers, closed its gates in panic, and made futile attempts to defend itself. In regard to these and many other details surrounding the fall of Nineveh, God permitted Nahum to look clearly and accurately into the future. The Lord wanted his people to know exactly what he was about to do.

Once again—this time for the final time in his prophecy—Nahum connected the destruction of Nineveh with the salvation and restoration of God's people. Assyria deserved God's vengeance, and it was important for the people to be clear about that. But it was even more important for them to focus their attention on the deliverance the Lord was going to bring to them. The Lord had brought the Assyrian armies—as his instruments and the rod of his anger—against Israel and Judah to punish his faithless people, and the resulting destruction had been severe. Huge amounts of tribute money had been paid to the Assyrians. Israelite hostages had been deported to faraway places, never to see their homes or their families again. Furthermore, the Assyrian forces had systematically devastated the land. Grape vines, fruit trees, olive trees—all which had taken years to nurture and grow—had all been stripped of their fruit and cut down. The Assyrians had destroyed other crops as well. They had not just plundered Judah's wealth; they had left its people in desperate straits, often on the verge of starvation. Now all of that would end. The Lord was about to restore his people.

> ³ **The shields of his soldiers are red;**
> **the warriors are clad in scarlet.**
> **The metal on the chariots flashes**
> **on the day they are made ready;**
> **the spears of pine are brandished.**
> ⁴ **The chariots storm through the streets,**
> **rushing back and forth through the squares.**
> **They look like flaming torches;**
> **they dart about like lightning.**

Nahum's style of writing becomes very vivid here. He uses short, crisp sentences and phrases to capture the sights and sounds of Nineveh's frantic but futile efforts to survive. The picture he paints is one filled with frenzied activity. The question that arises, however, is *Whose activity?* Is Nahum describing the fury of the battle charge of the Medes and Babylonians as they attack Nineveh and its suburbs? Or is he attempting to portray the frantic defensive preparations of the Assyrians as they struggle to get into position to fight for Nineveh? Or could it be that Nahum is describing the actions of both sides—perhaps describing the army of the Medes and Babylonians approaching (verse 3) and then describing the Assyrians as they run to man their defensive positions (verse 4)? The author of this commentary sees all the activity Nahum describes as being that of the Medes and Babylonians as they race through the suburbs to the walls of the city, begin their attack, and then take the city.

Out of all the many things that are occurring as the Medes and Babylonians approach the outskirts of Nineveh, Nahum focuses upon a color, the color red. The prophet Ezekiel informs us that red was the predominant color used by Chaldean (Babylonian) soldiers: "But she [Judah] carried her prostitution still further. She saw men portrayed on a wall, figures of Chaldeans portrayed in red, with belts around their waists and flowing turbans on their heads; all of them looked like Babylonian chariot officers, natives of Chaldea" (23:14,15). They also had a habit of painting their shields red. Xenophon, the Greek military historian of a later age, reports that the Medes were also accustomed to wearing red in battle. In addition to their red battle dress, the sun shining down on the metal parts of the chariots of this vast attacking army gave off a reddish reflection. The cypress spears being waved back and forth by the attacking infantry looked like a forest of pine trees above the red masses moving toward the city. So Nahum sees a sea of red—blood red—flowing irresistibly toward Nineveh. What an awe-inspiring impression this must have left on the hearts and minds of the city's defenders, striking terror into the heart of every Assyrian—soldier and citizen alike.

Another thing that catches Nahum's attention in the vision the Lord gives him is the speed at which the enemy army approaches. He sees chariots dashing around on the roads leading to and from Nineveh. These chariots served as the advance guard of the attacking army—rushing back and forth between the defensive lines of the Assyrians and their own troops, reporting where pockets of resistance or military outposts were located or where the Assyrians were preparing to draw up their battle lines. The chariots would also lead the first wave of attack through the streets and intersections of the villages and suburbs outside the city walls. To Nahum's eyes, they move so fast that they seem like streaks of lightning. As a time-exposure photograph of cars at night on a freeway causes headlights to appear as streaks of light, so the swiftly moving chariots appeared as mere indistinct blurs of motion.

The sense that Nahum would have us get from this description, of course, is the speed at which the Medes and Babylonians would approach Nineveh. All resistance to this lightninglike attack would be quickly overcome, barely slowing down their arrival at the city walls. Gone would be the might of the Assyrian army, which had terrorized the nations for so long. Not only would that army not advance into the suburbs and countryside to drive off the intruder, it wouldn't even be able to hold its own ground. In panic the Assyrian soldiers would rush for the city walls, hoping to find safety there.

> ⁵ **He summons his picked troops,**
>   **yet they stumble on their way.**
> **They dash to the city wall;**
>   **the protective shield is put in place.**
> ⁶ **The river gates are thrown open**
>   **and the palace collapses.**

Once again, the troops Nahum mentions are not specifically identified, but it certainly makes good sense to understand him to be speaking of the army attacking Nineveh. The king of the Medes would be choosing "his picked troops," his elite divisions, to make this attack. His Babylonian counterpart would do the same. Having taken all the outposts and suburbs of Nineveh, they are now ready to assault the city walls themselves. Their troops are so eager that they stumble over one another as they compete to be the first to reach the wall and begin the siege of Nineveh. Once the troops have encircled the city, the "protective shield" is put in place. These were wooden, reed, or wicker canopies that besieging armies set up over their battering rams and other siege equipment to protect themselves as they engaged in undermining or breaching the wall. These shields afforded some protection from the arrows, stones, and hot liquids that defenders showered upon the attackers in an effort to drive them off.

The capital city of the kingdom of Israel, Samaria, was not nearly as rich and powerful a city as Nineveh. It couldn't afford the kind of protection that Nineveh could. Yet, we are told that Samaria held out under siege by the Assyrians for three years (2 Kings 17:5). Likewise when Jerusalem was besieged by the Babylonians, it held out for a year and a half before it was brought to its knees. The writer of 2 Kings tells us,

> In the ninth year of Zedekiah's reign, on the tenth day of the tenth month, Nebuchadnezzar king of Babylon marched against Jerusalem with his whole army. He encamped outside the city and built siege works all around it. The city was kept under siege until the eleventh year of King Zedekiah. By the ninth day of the fourth month the famine in the city had become so severe that there was no food for the people to eat. (25:1-3)

And the city of Babylon, which was comparable in size and defenses to Nineveh, rebelled against Assyria when Ashurbanipal was king. For over a year it resisted Ashurbanipal's army, even though that army possessed the most advanced siege equipment in the ancient world.

Besieging a well-fortified city was usually not a quick procedure. It was a slow, drawn-out process that strained the patience and resources of the besieger as well as those who lived in the besieged city. Yet ancient historical records tell us that Nineveh, the most powerful and well-defended city of its day, fell to besieging armies in only three months. How did that happen?

Nahum may be giving us the answer in these verses. Here, and later in verse 8 of this chapter, Nahum speaks about the part that water would play in the fall of Nineveh, and flooding did play a major role in hastening the city's demise, just as Nahum predicted that it would. When Sennacherib made Nineveh the capital of the Assyrian Empire a century before its fall, he needed to increase the water supply—not only to take care of the growing population of the city but also to provide for the large parks and formal gardens he had built. Although Nineveh was built right on the banks of the Tigris River, its water was unfit for drinking. Fortunately, there was a small tributary that ran through the city. This was the Khosr. However, it often ran dry in the summer just when the demand for water was at its peak. To solve the problem, Sennacherib constructed channels and aqueducts that led from mountain streams down to the Khosr. He then dammed up the river outside the city. A reservoir with built-in flood gates held the water until it was needed. With this project Sennacherib accomplished a major engineering feat for his day. However, he also had inadvertently created a major weakness in Nineveh's defenses.

Nahum foresaw that at the beginning of the siege, the attacking armies would capture the floodgates of the Khosr upstream from Nineveh and throw them wide open, sending a deluge of water rushing down toward the city. The water in its rush to get downstream would then undermine the foundations of the walls, which were made of mud bricks and were easily destroyed by the rushing water. Both at the river gate where the Khosr entered the city and at the gate where it left, there would be serious damage to the adjacent walls. The damage would be bad enough that the wall near the gate would collapse, leaving gaping holes through which the invaders would have easy access to the city. Nahum also mentions that the palace built next to the Khosr would collapse when the floodwaters would wash away its foundations. (Nahum is not the only one to speak of water in connection with Nineveh's fall. A Greek historian, Diodorus, also preserves a tradition that a flood collapsed part of the wall during the siege of the city.)

Here is one of many examples in the Bible that impress us because of the accuracy of the prophecy—even down to minute details—that the Lord gives his prophet. To many unbelievers, the prophet's very accuracy serves as proof that he could not have written his book before the event itself took place. Nahum, they would argue, must be describing something that had already happened, because no one could possibly see that clearly into the future. But why shouldn't the Lord be able to give his prophets such accurate details? He controls the future. He creates the future. Nineveh would fall when he decreed and in the exact way he decreed.

> ⁷ **It is decreed that the city**
> **be exiled and carried away.**
> **Its slave girls moan like doves**
> **and beat upon their breasts.**
> ⁸ **Nineveh is like a pool,**
> **and its water is draining away.**

> "Stop! Stop!" they cry,
>   but no one turns back.
> 9 Plunder the silver!
>   Plunder the gold!
> The supply is endless,
>   the wealth from all its treasures!
> 10 She is pillaged, plundered, stripped!
>   Hearts melt, knees give way,
>   bodies tremble, every face grows pale.

Nahum now describes the devastating results of Nineveh's walls being breached. The NIV translators expressed some reservations about the meaning of the opening word of verse 7. They translated it as "It is decreed" and followed that by adding the words "the city," thereby designating what is the subject of the decree. "The city" does not occur in the Hebrew text.

Other commentators feel that the Hebrew word whose meaning is uncertain actually is a proper name for the Assyrian queen. If that assumption is correct, then Nahum is prophesying that the queen, together with her handmaidens, will possibly suffer the shame of exile and slavery in a foreign land. Whatever the case, Nahum's message is clear: Nineveh, either as a city or in the person of its queen, will suffer the very same fate that its armies had so frequently inflicted upon the populace and royalty of the many other capitals of the conquered nations that comprised its empire. The king is not mentioned here in connection with Ninevites being led into exile, and history records that Sin-shar-ishkun, the son of Ashurbanipal, died in the fire that completed the destruction of his palace. In his worst nightmares Ashurbanipal would never have imagined that his son would suffer such a fate just 14 years after his own death.

The landscape of the now-captured city would also be a sight to behold. Flood waters bring chaos to a city. They leave behind an ugly mess. That would also be the case in Nineveh as the surging waters of the Khosr receded. Many of the city's buildings were made of mud brick. Such building do not fare well in a flood; they dissolve into a shapeless mass. The beautiful trees and other garden plants that the kings of Nineveh had pointed to as their pride and joy would be uprooted and lie where the raging waters deposited them, like unsightly piles of rubbish.

The water would not be the only thing that drained away from the ravished city. The people, including soldiers, would flee the city as well, like rats deserting a sinking ship. What loyal defenders were still left in the city would try to stop them, but Assyrian soldiers would be deaf to the commands of their officers. Panic would set in. It would be no more possible to hold back the fleeing masses of fugitives than it would have been to hold back the floodwaters that had surged through the city. All would be lost!

When a city fell to its enemies, as Nineveh did, it lay wide open for looting and plundering. And what a place Nineveh would be for pillage and plunder! Throughout its history Assyria had plundered other people, draining the nations they defeated of their resources. In the process Nineveh became the richest city of the ancient Near East. For example, when Tiglath-Pileser III, the king of Assyria from 745 to 727, invaded Samaria in 743 B.C., the Israelite king Menahem bought him off with a thousand talents of silver (2 Kings 15:19,20). Think about it. That's roughly 37 tons of silver! Every wealthy Israelite man had to contribute one and a quarter pounds of silver to make up that enormous amount. Forty-two years later when Sennacherib invaded Judah, Hezekiah was forced to give him more than ten tons of silver and a ton of gold (2 Kings 18:13-15).

In his account of the Judean campaign, Sennacherib boasts, "I drove out 200,150 people [which were very profitable to sell as slaves], young and old, male and female, horses, mules, donkeys, camels, big and small cattle beyond counting, and considered them booty." These were the "profits" accumulated from only parts of two Assyrian campaigns. Tiglath-Pileser fought against other kings besides Menahem in 743 B.C. Sennacherib subdued other rebel countries besides Judah in 701 B.C. Each country had to pay exorbitant amounts to escape destruction, and in some cases certain levels of tribute were expected year after year.

Add to those amounts the taxes Assyria collected from its citizens, plus the annual tribute it got from the subject nations that made up its empire, and you have an almost unimaginable amount of wealth. Now it's true that not all of this wealth came to the capital city of Nineveh, but plenty of it did. Precious metals, livestock, war materials, clothing, utensils, and stores of other goods were carried into the city regularly and stored in the temples, palaces, and storehouses of the city. Nahum was not exaggerating when he spoke about the "endless" supply of gold and silver that would be open to plunder by the invaders once Nineveh was captured. Thousands of people would also be available as slaves. (Jonah says that 120,000 people lived in the city in 800 B.C., which was before the real glory years of Nineveh.) Note that Nahum promises that Nineveh would suffer the same fate it had inflicted on all the nations it had conquered. Nineveh's "wealth"—whether in the form of gold or silver or people who would be sold as slaves—would be seized, and when the invading looters, ransackers, and plunderers were done, there wouldn't be anything left. The city would be stripped clean.

A lion's den

¹¹ **Where now is the lions' den,**
    the place where they fed their young,
where the lion and lioness went,
    and the cubs, with nothing to fear?
¹² **The lion killed enough for his cubs**
    and strangled the prey for his mate,
filling his lairs with the kill
    and his dens with the prey.

¹³ **"I am against you,"**
    declares the LORD **Almighty.**
"I will burn up your chariots in smoke,
    and the sword will devour your young lions.
    I will leave you no prey on the earth.
The voices of your messengers
    will no longer be heard."

Nahum closes his description of Nineveh's destruction with what is called a "taunt song." Using that name for these verses is not meant to imply that the Lord is here inspiring his prophet to make fun of the fallen Assyrians as they face the Lord's anger. That would contradict the Lord's own command that his people love their enemies (Romans 12:14-21) and his assertion that he takes no pleasure in the death of the wicked (Ezekiel 18:32). What the prophet is ridiculing is Nineveh's reliance upon its own strength. That city's rulers took great pride in their military muscle and what they had achieved. The prophet Isaiah quotes these words spoken by Assyrian kings as being typical of their arrogance: "By the strength of my hand I have done this, and by my wisdom, because I have understanding. I removed the boundaries of nations, I plundered their treasures; like a mighty one I subdued their kings. As one reaches into a nest, so my hand reached for the wealth of the nations; as men gather abandoned eggs, so I gathered all the countries; not one flapped a wing, or opened its mouth to chirp" (10:13,14). Their arrogance flew in the face of the Lord's honor. When Nahum taunts the Assyrians, he, in a negative way, is asserting that all honor and praise belong to the Lord who rules over the affairs of all nations—even the mighty ones who defy his lordship.

Today we are accustomed to calling the lion "the king of beasts." The ancients viewed this animal in the same way. The lion is a mighty and majestic beast, confident and unafraid. Animals, like the rabbit, that frequently serve as prey for other animals are always on the alert, always afraid that some enemy is sneaking up on them. Not so the lion! If he wishes to sleep, he lies down right out in the open. He knows that no other animal dares to disturb him, much less attack him. No wonder the Assyrians admired the lion. They set up statues of lions throughout the country and frequently featured pictures of them on their reliefs and decorations. Assyrian kings hunted lions, believing that if they killed one, the spirit of the beast would become one with theirs. And some proud Assyrian monarchs spoke of themselves symbolically as lions. In his taunt Nahum uses the lion to represent Nineveh—an apt description for a military power known for its self-assured behavior, its ferocity, and its lack of pity. The Assyrians would have been pleased with the comparison.

Nahum moves on to a second point of comparison between the lion and Assyria. The lion's activities and feeding habits also provide a fitting picture of Assyria's violent greed—its lust for wealth and loot and plunder. Nahum describes the lion as ripping its victims apart and cramming its lair, or cave, full with their remains. Cities that resisted the Assyrian attack were torn apart and leveled to the ground. People were snatched out of their homeland and hauled away into exile in Assyria's den. Assyrian records boast of the vast amounts of plunder and tribute taken from its unfortunate opponents, and still the lust for more booty went on. It was never satisfied. Like lion caves filled with the ripped carcasses of the lion's prey, the great palaces and temples of Nineveh overflowed with the plunder that the Assyrians had brought home from their voracious expeditions of conquest.

Still the Assyrian lion was not content. He went out and kept on hunting—always looking for more prey, always trying to satisfy his own never-ending appetite, always trying to keep his hungry cubs and lioness happy. Living off the plundered wealth of others, the people of Nineveh had become accustomed to a high lifestyle. To feed that lifestyle the Assyrian lion had to continue hunting. He no longer hunted just for what he needed to stay alive. He hunted just to take and take and take.

Now the unheard of would happen. The lion (Assyria) was not only to be driven from the field, but its very den (Nineveh) was to be destroyed. "I will leave you no prey on the earth," the Lord declares. This does not mean that the ravenous Assyrian armies would run out of prey, other countries to conquer. Rather the lion, the predator, the conqueror, would be exterminated. The Assyrian lion would be wiped off the face of the earth. Nineveh, once as safe and secure and as formidable as a "lions' den" would now stand impotent and powerless—its "young lions" slain by "the sword." In short, Assyria would now become prey for others. This great feat would be the result of the Lord's judgment upon Nineveh, as the prophet had indicated so clearly in his earlier words.

Nahum closes this chapter by abandoning the lion imagery in order to talk about the Assyrian ambassadors who represented the king in foreign lands. Their voices had always been heard in foreign courts—bringing demands from the Assyrian monarch, demanding submission to Assyria, demanding that tribute be sent to Nineveh. Now their imperious voices would fall silent. Their demands would no longer be heard. The silence would be most welcome in any country, like Judah, that had grown tired of living under the oppressive thumb of Assyria.

The cause of the city's fall

3 Woe to the city of blood,
   full of lies,
full of plunder,
   never without victims!
² The crack of whips,
   the clatter of wheels,
galloping horses
   and jolting chariots!
³ Charging cavalry,
   flashing swords
   and glittering spears!
Many casualties,
   piles of dead,
bodies without number,
   people stumbling over the corpses—
⁴ all because of the wanton lust of a harlot,
   alluring, the mistress of sorceries,
who enslaved nations by her prostitution
   and peoples by her witchcraft.

Stylistically, Nahum is the leader among the minor prophets. In the opening verses of this chapter (much as he did in chapter 2, especially verses 1 and 9), Nahum uses short, staccato phrases—perhaps better described as crisp, intense outbursts, full of emotion and action—to record the final assault that will lead to Nineveh's doom. Once again, the chariots are in the forefront of the battle, with "the crack of whips, the clatter of wheels, [and] galloping horses." Drivers lash their horses, and the final charge has begun. The "jolting chariots" give way to the "charging cavalry" and to the infantry with their "flashing swords and glittering spears." The result? "Piles of [Assyrian] dead, bodies without number, people stumbling over the corpses." Mighty Nineveh has fallen. That's the big picture. Now let's back up for the details.

The "city of blood" mentioned in the opening verse is clearly Nineveh. Nahum further describes it as "full of plunder, never without victims." Nahum is not exaggerating when he calls Nineveh a "city of blood." Assyrian war tactics are regarded as some of the most cruel and bloodthirsty of all history. Countries and cities that refused to surrender to Assyrian demands often found their leaders skinned alive or impaled on sharpened posts. Officers in opposing armies had their limbs cut off, their tongues and teeth pulled out, their eyes gouged out, or their heads lopped off. These body parts were then piled up before the city gates as an object lesson for all to see, or their corpses were stacked like cords of firewood as a clear and most visible warning of what would happen if anyone else would dare to challenge their Assyrian lords. Sometimes the entire population of a certain city was burned to death—men, women, and children.

Armies today try to hide the atrocities they commit and deny that they ever took place. The kings of Nineveh, however, boasted about such things. They believed that the news about these gory deeds would discourage people from rebelling against them. But by Nahum's time such bloody practices served no purpose at all. Yet Ashurbanipal still indulged in them simply to satisfy his lust for blood. One could liken the Assyrians to a man-eater—an animal that has tasted human blood and now needs more and more to satisfy its craving. Because the habits of a man-eater can't be reversed, such animals are destroyed. The same would hold true for blood-crazed Assyria. The Lord would destroy her. The victims of the bloody city were now to be avenged.

Nahum mentions a second reason why God's divine judgment was about to fall on Nineveh. The city was a place of deception, "full of lies," just like any center of corrupt human power. In order to get enemy cities to surrender without a full-scale siege, Assyrian generals often made promises to the inhabitants that they had no intention of keeping. Here's a typical example: When Sennacherib's armies surrounded Jerusalem, the Assyrian general used these alluring words to try to get the city to surrender:

> Do not listen to Hezekiah. This is what the king of Assyria says: Make peace with me and come out to me. Then every one of you will eat from his own vine and fig tree and drink water from his own cistern, until I come and take you to a land like your own, a land of grain and new wine, a land of bread and vineyards, a land of olive trees and honey. Choose life and not death!

> Do not listen to Hezekiah, for he is misleading you when he says, "The LORD will deliver us." (2 Kings 18:31,32)

Such fine sounding words were intended to cover up the truth—the cruel way Assyria customarily dealt with rebellious cities. They were lies designed to help the Assyrians get what they wanted. Throughout history, nations have used lies and half-truths in order to secure an advantage at the expense of some other nation or individual.

Nahum goes on to describe the real motivating force behind Assyrian activities, and in the process gives another reason why the Lord's judgment would fall upon Nineveh. The city and its rulers were driven by "the wanton lust of a harlot." Nahum compares the city to a deceitful prostitute who uses her charms and enticements to trick other people into trusting her and then takes them for whatever they have. In most cases she is willing to do anything, moral or immoral, to get what she wants. This image accurately described Assyria. Assyria was willing to lie, cheat, rob, and murder in order to satisfy her bloated appetite. By her military and commercial policies, she beguiled nations into forfeiting their independence. All of this had but one aim: to satisfy her lust for more wealth and power—for world supremacy. The city of Nineveh looked beautiful on the outside. No doubt it attracted people from throughout the world to its culture and power. But its desires were those of a harlot, and those who united themselves with the city joined her in her harlotry.

The harlot city is further called "the mistress of sorceries." This brings the heathen practices of Assyrian idol worship into the picture. Assyrian idolatry could well be labeled harlotry, because there were immoral elements involved in the worship of the love-goddess, Ishtar, after whom Nineveh was named. But nothing was more characteristic of that religion than witchcraft and sorcery. Like many heathens, the Assyrians believed the world was filled with evil spirits that had to be appeased and from which a person had to seek protection. With rituals, amulets, magic formulas, love potions, charms, and spells—all part of the harlot's stock in trade—they sought to protect themselves, insure the future, and direct the power of evil against their enemies.

No Assyrian king would ever begin a military campaign or undertake a project without first consulting an astrologer or finding a favorable omen among the entrails of an animal. His subjects followed the same practice in their private lives. The description of King Ahaz' contacts with Assyria

(2 Kings 16) shows what Nahum means when he says that others had been misled and enslaved by what they assumed to be the power of Assyrian witchcraft. The sorcery of Nineveh played a significant role in the unfaithfulness that the people of Judah often displayed toward the one true God of heaven and earth.

Citizens of our day and age look upon the superstitious practices of the Assyrians as foolishness. How could the Assyrians get caught up in them? How could Israel and Judah be so easily deceived by them? Condescending questions like that, however, often overlook similar situations that lie closer to home. Some modern people, even God's people, wear lucky charms today. After having some success while wearing a certain pair of socks during a sporting event, an athlete will wear those same socks in the next game, hoping that the initial success will repeat itself. Many people feel uneasy about staying on the 13th floor of a hotel; they feel much better if the hotel management gives the floor a different number—even though, of course, it still physically remains the 13th floor. If something unpleasant is known to have happened in a certain house, people avoid that place lest the evil "dwelling there" harms them too.

Superstition is foolishness! Superstition is unreasonable! But superstition continues to exert a powerful influence today, just as it did in ancient times. God's people, ancient and modern, however, know and confess by the way they live that they are in the hands of a loving God who has made them his own in Jesus Christ. What happens to them in the future does not depend on possessing good luck, avoiding bad luck, or controlling good and evil spirits. The present and future belong to the Lord of heaven and earth. They are his to control and use for the good of his people.

⁵ "I am against you," declares the LORD Almighty.
   "I will lift your skirts over your face.
  I will show the nations your nakedness
    and the kingdoms your shame.
⁶ I will pelt you with filth,
    I will treat you with contempt
    and make you a spectacle.
⁷ All who see you will flee from you and say,
    'Nineveh is in ruins—who will mourn for her?'
   Where can I find anyone to comfort you?"

Again the Lord makes his attitude toward Nineveh perfectly clear. As a holy God, as a jealous God, he cannot and will not tolerate sins like those committed by Nineveh. He was "against" Nineveh and everything it stood for. If Nineveh insisted on acting like a prostitute, then he would treat it like one. At times in the ancient world, women convicted of prostitution were paraded down the street naked or with their robes lifted up over their heads so that they would experience the public shame and humiliation of having their fellow townspeople view their nakedness. The people who watched them go by pelted them with manure or dirt or almost anything else that could be found to throw at them. This scene of contempt and ridicule portrays Nineveh's ultimate disgrace. The city that had disgraced others will now be exposed for what she was and then shamefully disgraced. What a downfall for the proud and haughty city.

Even in a world where news was carried by fleet-footed messengers or hard-charging horseback riders, the word would spread like wildfire: "Nineveh is in ruins." There would be no television pictures transmitted by satellite to verify what the messengers had reported, and the peoples of far-off lands like Judah would find the reports of the messengers hard to believe. But as more and more reports came in, all consistently bringing the same news, the truth would finally sink in. The impossible had happened! The unlikely had taken place! The great, the powerful, the unassailable city had fallen!

Then great Nineveh would find out how many friends and allies she really had. While she was the mistress of the world, she might have thought that she had plenty. After all, her streets were always full of traders and merchants from foreign lands. Visitors from all over that part of the world flocked to her attractions and marveled at her beauty. Ambassadors from many lands crowded into her palaces and bowed respectfully before her rulers. To judge by appearances, she was highly popular, even loved by the world around her. How that world would grieve if the impossible actually happened and she were to disappear! But, as Nahum points out, appearances can be deceiving.

The adoration was all external. In fact, it covered up the fear and hatred and resentment in the hearts of those who bowed or cowered before her. The people of the lands around Assyria hated Nineveh for what she had done to them. They hoped and prayed for her destruction and an end to her dominance over them. So when the message "Nineveh has fallen" went out, not a single tear would be shed. No friend would come forward to comfort the city. No ally would attempt to relieve her pain. Comfort and relief would belong to those who had been released from Nineveh's iron clutches—not to the city sitting in ashes. Nineveh would die alone.

> **⁸ Are you better than Thebes,**
>   **situated on the Nile,**
>   **with water around her?**
> **The river was her defense,**
>   **the waters her wall.**
> **⁹ Cush and Egypt were her boundless strength;**
>   **Put and Libya were among her allies.**

¹⁰ **Yet she was taken captive**
and went into exile.
Her infants were dashed to pieces
at the head of every street.
Lots were cast for her nobles,
and all her great men were put in chains.

Nahum closes this final chapter of his book in the same way he ended the previous chapter, with a taunt song. Again the purpose of this song is not to ridicule a fallen enemy but to condemn the sinful pride of Nineveh. (See the commentary on the closing verses of chapter 2 for a fuller explanation of the taunt song.)

In case anyone (the Assyrians included) thought that Nahum's prophecy about the destruction of Nineveh was a figment of his imagination, Nahum reminds his readers of what had happened to another seemingly all-powerful and indestructible city. He compares Nineveh to the ancient Egyptian city of Thebes. Located in the southern part of Egypt on the upper reaches of the Nile River, Thebes was the capital of ancient Egypt throughout much of its history as well as a leading center of Egyptian civilization (represented today by the impressive ruins at Luxor and the Valley of the Kings). Under the pharaohs who lived at Thebes, Egypt had annexed the kingdom of Cush to the south. Because the city and the surrounding territory it controlled were so strong, other nations in the vicinity, like Libya and Put, had cast their lot with Thebes. Their combined military strength made Thebes a world class power.

The citizens of Thebes thought they had every reason to feel secure. Their city was built like a fortress, with thick walls. It was surrounded by loyal friends and allies. The city itself was strategically located, surrounded by water. It was situated hundreds of miles up the Nile, far away from all its potential enemies. It took a five hundred mile march through practically the entire land of Egypt just to reach it. Could their situation be any more ideal? Surely, this was one city that would never fall and be plundered by its foes.

Ironically, it was none other than Assyria and her armies which showed Thebes how unfounded its confidence was. In 675 B.C. Esarhaddon was the first king of Nineveh to attack Egypt. After four years of campaigning, he gained control of northern Egypt in the delta region of the Nile, but the effect was short-lived. When the Assyrian armies left, the Egyptians soon regained control of their own affairs.

After Esarhaddon's death in 667 B.C., his son Ashurbanipal renewed the attempt to conquer Egypt. Again the Assyrian armies were successful, and Egypt pledged its allegiance to Assyria. But this allegiance lasted only as long as the Assyrian armies were present to enforce it. For Ashurbanipal to fulfill his dream of making Egypt a part of the Assyrian Empire, it became necessary for him to return once more. This time Ashurbanipal was determined to bring Thebes to its knees. He drove all the way up the Nile, leaving behind a horrifying trail of fire and ruin, to say nothing of all the dead and mutilated Egyptian soldiers and civilians—men, women, and children.

Finally he arrived at Thebes itself. The city that had depended so much on its distance from its enemies suddenly stood face-to-face with an opposing army. For all her strength and vaunted defenses, the city fell to the Assyrians in 663 B.C. Nahum describes the horrors of war that Ashurbanipal unleashed upon Thebes' citizens. Its wealth—which had seemed so safe a short time before—became plunder for the Assyrian war machine. Its infants were taken out into the streets and were dashed to pieces. Its nobles were sold as personal slaves to individual conquerors. Its upper classes—trained and educated men—were put in chains and dragged away to be used in the service of their Assyrian captors. And the rest of the people who survived the war were deported to Assyria as prisoners of war, destined to spend the rest of their lives as slaves. Then Asurbanipal leveled the city to the ground. How mighty Assyria and haughty Nineveh must have scoffed at the false security Thebes had placed in its remote location, its walls, and its armies and powerful allies.

> **¹¹ You too will become drunk;**
> **you will go into hiding**
> **and seek refuge from the enemy.**
>
> **¹² All your fortresses are like fig trees**
> **with their first ripe fruit;**
> **when they are shaken,**
> **the figs fall into the mouth of the eater.**
> **¹³ Look at your troops—**
> **they are all women!**
> **The gates of your land**
> **are wide open to your enemies;**
> **fire has consumed their bars.**

It's ironic how Nineveh could see the blindness of Thebes to its vulnerability and yet not recognize that she herself was afflicted in the same way. Nahum prophesies that what happened to Thebes was going to happen to Nineveh. Some 50 years after Nineveh brought tears to the citizens of Thebes, she would be weeping for herself. That anything like this ever could happen must have seemed impossible in the days of Ashurbanipal, when Nahum wrote—but his words turned out to be true nonetheless. They turned out to be true—not because Nahum made a lucky guess or because he could see the handwriting on the wall better than others, but because Nahum was speaking the Lord's words. Furthermore, the

Lord was not merely predicting the future. He was laying out his blueprint for the future, one he himself would carry out without fail.

Nineveh's sense of security was just as ill-founded as that of Thebes. Nahum prophesies that its vaunted defenses will be shown to be worthless. Merely "shaking" them will cause them to fall, the way ripe figs are easily shaken from the tree and fall into the mouth of the person below, who then devours them. And the Assyrian soldiers, once renowned for their fighting ability, will reveal themselves to be weak and spineless. Instead of defending the city, they will flee for their lives, leaving the city gates wide open when they go. The enemy will find no resistance. The people of the city will cower in caves, hoping the enemy soldiers will not find them. The only relief for the peoples' fear and terror will be found in drunkenness. Strong drink will dull their senses and make them incapable of facing up to the terrible reality. Can't you just imagine the Assyrian soldiers in crude mockery saying the same thing about the people of Thebes only five decades earlier?

> ¹⁴ **Draw water for the siege,**
> **strengthen your defenses!**
> **Work the clay,**
> **tread the mortar,**
> **repair the brickwork!**
> ¹⁵ **There the fire will devour you;**
> **the sword will cut you down**
> **and, like grasshoppers, consume you.**
> **Multiply like grasshoppers,**
> **multiply like locusts!**
> ¹⁶ **You have increased the number of your merchants**
> **till they are more than the stars of the sky,**
> **but like locusts they strip the land**
> **and then fly away.**

¹⁷ **Your guards are like locusts,**
   your officials like swarms of locusts
   that settle in the walls on a cold day—
but when the sun appears they fly away,
   and no one knows where.

Once again, as he had done at the beginning of chapter 2, Nahum challenges the city to get ready for battle, to get ready for the siege. Water must be drawn and stored before the enemy cuts off the supply of drinking water by stopping up the Khosr River. Bricks must be made to fortify the weak spots in the 50-foot wide walls. Lots of work, hard work, must be done, but it would all be in vain. Even the all-out efforts of the Ninevites would postpone the destruction for only a few months at best. In the end, "fire" and "sword" would "devour" and "consume" the inhabitants of the city, much as grasshoppers devour and consume everything in their path.

Two very prominent and important components of Nineveh's society are mentioned by Nahum: merchants and government officials (including the military). The city's strength was built on its military and commercial activities. But these people—once the heart and soul of its strength and the driving force behind its expansionist policies—would fail Nineveh in its death agony. The merchants, "like locusts," would "strip the land," grabbing as much wealth as they could on their way out of town. The officials, in their rush to leave the doomed city, would add to the chaos rather than calming the people and rallying them to defend the city—as was their duty. All of them, merchants and officials alike, would desert the crumbling city like rats deserting a sinking ship.

Nahum then uses an illustration involving locusts to make another significant point. If you've ever wondered where all the bugs—so plenteous in summer—disappear to in winter, then you get Nahum's picture. In Nahum's day, locusts were so bountiful in Assyria and Israel that clouds of them blocked out the light of the sun at times. Hordes of locusts would descend on a country and strip its fields bare in a matter of hours. Then they would disappear as if they had never been there. Nahum compares their behavior to that of the Assyrian merchants and officials who were responsible for stripping the countries around them. There were so many officials on government business, so many merchants on the roads of Israel who called Nineveh home, and yet, like the locusts, they would all suddenly disappear. Why? This is what the Lord had decreed for Nineveh. Its society, which seemed so stable, so indestructible, and so huge, would vanish like insects roused by the summer heat.

> **[18] O king of Assyria, your shepherds slumber;**
> **your nobles lie down to rest.**
> **Your people are scattered on the mountains**
> **with no one to gather them.**
> **[19] Nothing can heal your wound;**
> **your injury is fatal.**
> **Everyone who hears the news about you**
> **claps his hands at your fall,**
> **for who has not felt**
> **your endless cruelty?**

When the end did come, there would no mystery as to the whereabouts of the officials and rulers and nobles ("shepherds") and people of Nineveh. Many of them, particularly the leaders and rulers, would "slumber" or "lie down to rest," that is, would be in their graves. The king himself, Sinsharishkun, one of Ashurbanipal's sons, would also lie down in death as his palace burned around him. The rest of the population that was fortunate enough to escape the massacre headed for the mountains to the east and north of

Nineveh. There, with no shepherds to guide them, they scattered helplessly like a flock of sheep. "No one" would ever "gather them" again.

This was it! There would be no reversing this calamity. Nineveh would never rise again. The destruction was permanent. At other times in its history Assyria had faced reversals. It had suffered setbacks, which at the time made it look as though Assyrian power was finished, but that had never happened. The empire always bounced back and went on to become even bigger and stronger than before. Now, however, things would be different. Nahum prophesies that this truly would be the end of Assyria and its capital. The wounds inflicted on Assyria were beyond cure. "Nothing can heal your wound; your injury is fatal." Assyria would never recover from this blow. The great city would lie in ruins forever. As usual, the Lord was true to his word. He never again allowed Nineveh to be anything more than a heap of dust and ashes. For centuries even its location was unknown.

Every nation in that part of the world had suffered from Assyria's cruel and brutal tactics, had been stomped upon by her iron boots, and had been forced to grovel under her authority. "For who has not felt your endless cruelty?" Nahum asks. So there were no tears when Nineveh fell. "Everyone who hears the news about you claps his hands at your fall." As Nineveh's victims celebrated its destruction, they clapped their hands in wild rejoicing, delighted that the tyrant had been slain, rejoicing that the proud and cruel city was gone. All the nations of the earth would eventually learn what had happened, but only those who listened to Nahum would know *why* it happened. They could confess, "The Lord has acted. He has poured out his vengeance upon his enemies, and in so doing, he has delivered his people."

Concluding thought

We would like to conclude this study by reminding ourselves of something we talked about already in the introduction to the book of Nahum. Nahum's book is remote to us
in many ways. The events he foretold happened so long
ago. And as far as most of us can tell, we aren't any better
off—or worse off, for that matter—because the city of Nineveh has disappeared. We have enough things in our own
age and in our own individual lives that concern us. How
can we possibly be concerned about or be moved in any
meaningful way by what happened in Israel and Nineveh
centuries ago?

When we entertain such questions, it's best to remember
how Nahum began his book. He described the one true God,
who is still the Lord of heaven and earth. He told us that the
Lord is a God of infinite patience who wants the sinner to be
saved, but who at the same time is a holy God who will not
let the wicked escape unpunished. The godless and haughty
nations of today have the same God to contend with as Nineveh did, and they can expect their contact with him to have
the same results if they continue to defy him.

The book of Nahum also emphasizes that there is a
reverse side to God's judgment upon his enemies. The *gracious eye of the Lord* is still upon his people today as well.
Though it may seem as though the people of God are
fighting a losing battle—being overwhelmed by a host of
enemies—the gates of hell will not prevail against the
Lord's church. We have his promise, the promise of the
God who made us, the promise of the God who redeemed
us. He can and will deliver today as he has done in the
past. The patience he shows to the wicked and to us
should never be misinterpreted as a lack of power or
resolve on his part. Here is the comfort the church of God

can draw from the book of Nahum, even in her darkest hours. The Lord, the Savior-God, has not stepped down from his position. He has not forgotten his people.

Certainly Nahum warns us about trusting in man-made structures and the power they possess. Strong and stable government is a blessing of God, but to place our sense of security and well-being solely in that institution itself is to misplace our trust. All is well with us because the Lord is God, and he rules heaven and earth. That God who has sealed his love for us in Christ will never leave us or forsake us. In quiet patience and confidence, the Lord's people wait for him to carry out his plans and unfold the future in his infinite wisdom and love.

Compare the final words of the previous paragraph with the last words of Nahum's prophecy. What a contrast! The closing words Nahum uses to describe Nineveh and the works of men: "endless cruelty." The final words that we can use to describe the Lord and his works: "wisdom and love."

INTRODUCTION TO HABAKKUK

Those readers who use computers for word processing know that one function of such programs allows the computer to check your spelling. If you use a word that's not in its dictionary, the computer will call your attention to that word and will even give some suggestions on what word you might have meant to use and how to spell it. If the computer can't recognize the word or even associate another word with it, the message "No Suggestions!" will appear on-screen. That's exactly what happens when you type the name *Habakkuk* into a computer—you get no suggestions. The name is equally strange to present-day Christians. No parents use it as a name for one of their children the way they do with the names of some of the other prophets. The message of the book, unfortunately, is as unfamiliar as his name to all too many.

Author

We know nothing about Habakkuk outside of what his book tells us, and that is very little. Nothing is said about his background—about where he came from or when he lived and worked. As noted above, even his name is strange—strange to the modern English-speaking reader and strange to the ancient Israelite as well. Some, like Luther, have suggested that Habakkuk's name comes from a Hebrew verb which means "to embrace," and so they interpret his name to mean "the comforter" or "the one who consoles." Others insist that Habakkuk is a foreign name, that it's an Assyrian word for a garden plant which was cultivated throughout the Middle East in ancient times. Whatever the origin of the name may be, Habakkuk is unknown to us outside his book.

There is, however, a legend that has grown up around Habakkuk. He is mentioned in the apocryphal addition to the book of Daniel called *Bel and the Dragon*. This book, like other books of the Apocrypha, was written in the time between the Old and New Testaments. According to the legend, Habakkuk was in Judea, taking food to some workers out in the fields. An angel appeared and told him to go to Babylon and give the food to Daniel instead. Daniel had already spent six days in the lion's den and was hungry. Habakkuk replied that he'd never been to Babylon and knew nothing about any lion's den. So the angel lifted him by the hair and took him there. After Habakkuk assisted Daniel in the lion's den, the angel returned Habakkuk once again to Judea. Interesting as this little apocryphal story may be, it doesn't really shed any light for us on Habakkuk as a person.

Habakkuk also may have been a Levite and a member of the choir that sang in the temple. His book ends with a psalm (chapter 3), one which is every bit as beautiful and well-written as those recorded in the book of Psalms. Habakkuk's psalm even begins with directions about the melody to be used when singing it. It also has the mysterious word "Selah" alongside it three times—the only times this word occurs in the Old Testament outside of the book of Psalms. Although Habakkuk may have been a Levite, a person *doesn't have to be* a professional musician in order to compose good music. Habakkuk, like King David, may have had talents in that area even though he didn't make his living doing it. Like many other things that have been proposed about Habakkuk, this too is speculation. There really is not a great deal we can say about the man's background with certainty.

Date

Habakkuk is also silent about the particular time when he wrote. He doesn't do what so many other prophets did—date his writing by the reign of a certain king of Israel or Judah. So those who want to figure out where Habakkuk fits in the Old Testament scheme of things have to depend upon clues the prophet gives us in his book. And there's really only one statement that is helpful in this respect. In 1:5,6, the Lord says through Habakkuk, "Look at the nations and watch—and be utterly amazed. For I am going to do something in your days that you would not believe, even if you were told. I am raising up the Babylonians."

The Lord foretells the coming of the Babylonians under King Nebuchadnezzar. According to the Lord's words, then, this prophecy was spoken at a time when what it foretold would be considered highly improbable. The Lord, in fact, indicates to Habakkuk that even after he has been told about it, Habakkuk and the people of his day would have a hard time believing it.

Yet, if one reads on further, it seems as though Habakkuk is familiar with the Babylonians and their warlike ways. This would seem to indicate a time when the Babylonians were already on the world scene but had not yet become such a powerful nation that anyone would have expected them to spread their influence as far as Canaan—some nine hundred miles from Babylon—and loom as a serious threat to the existence of Judah.

There is a period of time that seems to meet these qualifications. In 626 B.C., Babylon, under the leadership of Nabopolassar, Nebuchadnezzar's father, declared its indepen-

dence from Assyria. Nabopolassar (626–605 B.C.) was a
Chaldean, a chieftain of one of the tribes that had settled in
the land south of Babylon at least four centuries earlier. There
these Chaldeans constantly resisted the Assyrians' attempts to
dominate them. Finally, in 626 B.C., they turned the tables on
the Assyrians. In a battle fought outside the city of Babylon,
they won control over what had up till then been the Assyrian province of Babylon. Nabopolasser then took over the
throne of Babylon. This was the beginning of the Chaldean,
or New Babylonian, Empire. Babylon was never under the
control of the Assyrians again, but it still would not have
been obvious in 626 B.C. that the New Babylonian Empire
was eventually going to control all of Assyria's empire.

Then, in 612 B.C., the Babylonians and the Medes
marched into the Assyrian heartland itself and laid siege
to the city of Nineveh, the capital city of Assyria. Three
months later, Nineveh was burned to the ground, just as
the prophet Nahum had predicted. The remaining Assyrian forces scattered and headed west. They attempted to
regroup and make a stand at Haran, but in 610 B.C., the
Babylonians and their allies took Haran too. Now all of
Assyria was in their hands.

For centuries the Assyrians had been *the* superpower
in the Middle East. Now with the collapse of their empire,
there was a power vacuum in the region—a vacuum
which both the Babylonians and the Egyptians were only
too eager to fill. One of the prize pawns in this power
struggle would be the "bridge area" of Syria-Palestine that
lay directly between the two. (The Medes were content to
remain in control of the lands they had in the east.) So
after Nineveh fell, the Egyptians quickly marched north,
intending to contain any possible Babylonian expansion at
the Euphrates.

For seven years the Egyptians succeeded in holding the Babylonians in check at the Euphrates River. During that time it seemed highly unlikely that the Babylonians would ever be able to defeat the Egyptians, cross the Euphrates, move down the Mediterranean coast, and gain control over Syria and Palestine (including Judah)—at one time all parts of the vaunted Assyrian Empire.

All this ended in 605 B.C., however. Nabopolasser's son Nebuchadnezzar decisively defeated the Egyptians in a battle at Carchemish on the upper Euphrates River. This monumental victory solidified the New Babylonian Empire and established Babylon as the power to be reckoned with in the Middle East. The question of who would control areas west of the Euphrates was no longer in question.

That same year Nebuchadnezzar marched southward into the areas that had been controlled by Egypt to show that he was now in control. When he came to Jerusalem, he took some young men, including Daniel, from leading Jewish families back to Babylon with him as hostages. He also made it very clear that he was the ruler of all the former Assyrian Empire.

During those seven years before Carchemish (612–605 B.C.) the power of the Chaldeans was well-known, but their domination of Judah was still in the future. So the Lord could have spoken the way he did to Habakkuk sometime during those years. And since the godly Judean king Josiah was ruling during half of those years, it is usually assumed that the conditions Habakkuk complains about would have followed Josiah's death. The years of Josiah's son, Jehoiakim, were wicked ones—years of evil, impenitence, and violence. They match up well with Habakkuk's complaints.

This leaves a date for Habakkuk between 609 and 605 B.C. That would make him a younger contemporary of

Nahum and Zephaniah. This date also places him right in the middle of Jeremiah's ministry. He may even have served with Jeremiah for a number of years.

Form and content

The form of Habakkuk's book is unique among the prophets. The first two chapters are a dialogue between Habakkuk and God. Habakkuk's contributions to the conversation are the complaints he lodges with God—perhaps on behalf of the believers still left in Judah. The Lord, in turn, answers Habakkuk's questions. Having received his answer from God, Habakkuk responds and closes out his book with a beautiful psalm. This psalm shows us that Habakkuk has, in faith, accepted the Lord's answers to the soul-wrenching questions he had raised. At the same time it serves as a beautiful confession of faith—it expresses the confidence Habakkuk has in the Lord and the Lord's rule over the earth and all its inhabitants.

One of the things that makes Habakkuk's book so interesting and valuable and so worth studying is that he asks some of the really fundamental questions that God's people of every age have raised and still do. He asks, "Why?" If the Lord is a just God who hates evil, then why does he allow evil to fill the earth? Why do the wicked go unpunished? If the Lord is a loving God who cares for his people, then why does he allow them to suffer? Why does he allow them to experience evil in the world? These are extremely important questions for the spiritual well-being of believers. The wrong answer—or no answer at all—can drive God's children away from the faith and into bitterness, anger, and despair.

Habakkuk, however, not only asks the questions; he also provides an excellent model for believers to follow while they wait for God's answer. Habakkuk says, "I will look to see what he will say to me, and what answer I am to give to this complaint" (2:1). When Habakkuk stands before the Lord and voices his complaints, he is not out to challenge God or to start a debate with God about the way God rules the earth. No, he is looking for answers that he can take to the Lord's people—answers that will strengthen their faith and relieve the anxiety they had been experiencing.

Since this is the spirit in which Habakkuk approaches him, God graciously responds and shares his future plans with Habakkuk. He assures Habakkuk that evil has not escaped his notice, neither the evil in Judah nor that produced by the Babylonians. Wickedness will be punished, and no one will escape. These things *will* happen, but they will happen in the Lord's own good time.

These answers give substance to the theme of the book, "The righteous will live by his faith" (2:4). The Lord told Habakkuk what to expect in the near future, but he does not give a direct answer to the question, Why does the Lord tolerate evil? The evil of Judah will be punished by the evil of Babylon. The evil of Babylon will, in turn, be punished by another nation of evildoers. In addition, God's people will continue to suffer in this world.

So where then is the eternal justice of God? The Lord's answer is a call to faith. "Trust me" is the Lord's encouragement. That is what differentiates the Lord's people from unbelievers. Believers operate in the confidence that all is in the Lord's hands and that he is controlling all things for the good of the members of his eternal family. When that assurance rests in believers' hearts, they can join Habakkuk in the midst of calamity and say, "Yet I will wait patiently. . . . I will rejoice in the LORD, I will be joyful in God my Savior" (3:16,18).

The final chapter of Habakkuk is set in a form which indicates that it was probably used in public worship—perhaps in times of great calamity and disaster. We can take this as evidence that God's Spirit not only worked confidence in God in Habakkuk's heart but also worked that same confidence in the hearts of God's other children as well. In the days and weeks and years and perhaps even centuries that followed, believers made Habakkuk's words their own as they used his psalm in worship.

Outline

Theme: The righteous will live by faith

   I. The title (1:1)

  II. A dialogue about evil in the world (1:2–2:20)

     A. Habakkuk asks about evil in Judah (1:2-4)
     B. The Lord responds that the Babylonians will punish Judah (1:5-11)
     C. Habakkuk asks about evil among the Babylonians (1:12–2:1)
     D. The Lord responds that the Babylonian evil also will be punished (2:2-20)

  III. A psalm of faith in the Lord's justice and saving power (3:1-19)

     A. A call for the Lord to deliver as he has in the past (3:1-15)
     B. A confession of the Lord's gracious power to save (3:16-19)

PART ONE

The Title
(1:1)

1 **The oracle that Habakkuk the prophet received.**

The title gives us the author's name, Habakkuk, and that's really all he tells us about himself. He mentions no hometown or family tree. He lists no kings during whose reigns he lived and worked, nor is he mentioned in the historical books of the Old Testament that cover his time period, books like 2 Kings and 2 Chronicles. No other prophet mentions him either, even though he was a contemporary of Jeremiah and may have known Nahum and Zephaniah, who labored for the Lord shortly before he prophesied. Whatever we do know about him—his attitude, his faith, and the like—must be inferred from his book's content.

The title of Habakkuk's book also informs us that he received an "oracle" from the Lord. The Hebrew word that the NIV translates as "oracle" means "something which is lifted up." The term could imply that Habakkuk is being called upon to "lift up his voice" to reveal the truth of the Lord, or it could refer to some "heavy burden" (KJV translation) the prophet is being asked to lift up and carry or, perhaps, to deliver. Used in that way, the term usually indicates some message of doom and destruction that is about to be related or delivered by the prophet.

Other prophets who begin their books in much the same way are Nahum and Malachi, and Zechariah labels two of his prophecies as "oracles" (9:1; 12:1). Isaiah also uses the term frequently, especially in the section of his book where he pronounces doom on foreign nations (chapters 13–23).

The title also informs us that Habakkuk was a prophet. The image that comes to mind in connection with a man who's been labeled a "prophet" is that of a person who can foretell, or predict, the future. That's how the word *prophet* is used almost exclusively today, and Habakkuk can be understood as a prophet in that sense. God, you see, allowed Habakkuk a glimpse into the future. God enabled him then to foretell events—to let the people of Judah know, for example, that the Babylonians would come and punish them for their wickedness and that the Babylonians, in turn, would be punished for theirs.

Habakkuk was able to do this because the Lord himself revealed these things to him. Note that Habakkuk says that he had "received" this "oracle," or revelation, that he was now passing on to his readers. In other words, the Lord himself was the one who had revealed his plans for Judah's future to Habakkuk. He wanted his people to be prepared when the time came. So, as God's prophet, it became Habakkuk's responsibility to let the people of Judah know what God had revealed to him, to let them know what the future held for them.

The coming of the Babylonians began a dark period in Judah's history. Habakkuk's prophecy indicates that they invaded Judah because the Lord wanted it that way. So things were not out of the Lord's control when these fearsome enemies attacked Judah and overwhelmed the country. No, all these events unfolded exactly as the Lord—in his wise providence—had already determined that they would. Letting his prophets, like Habakkuk, foresee and reveal future events to the people before they happened was one way in which the Lord brought this truth home to his people.

Foretelling the future, however, was not the only function of God's prophets. In fact, it was not even their chief task or responsibility. Behind the Hebrew word for "prophet" lies the idea of "one who is appointed or called to speak." A prophet, then, is a person who has been summoned by God to speak for him—to serve as God's spokesman, God's mouthpiece. The prophet's first and foremost responsibility was to speak for God to the people—to communicate to them what God had revealed to him. Habakkuk does this when he brings God's special revelation about Judah and Babylon to the people.

A prophet's responsibility, however, went beyond speaking *to* the people *for* God. It also involved speaking *to* God *for* the people. Abraham—called a prophet in Genesis 20:7—*prayed* to God for the king of Gerar. Moses—at the time of the golden calf incident—*prayed* to God on behalf of the people gathered around Mount Sinai, pleading with him to forgive their unfaithfulness. In a similar way, Habakkuk took the complaints that the people were making about the way God was governing the affairs of Judah and the world and, on behalf of those people, brought their complaints and questions directly to the Lord.

A prophet might also *lead* his people in the way they ought to *pray and confess* before the Lord. Elijah did this on Mount Carmel when he challenged the prophets of Baal. Ezra did it after the exile when he led the people in worship. Habakkuk does it too in the final chapter of his book. The psalm recorded there contains both a prayer and a confession of faith. While that psalm began as a personal expression of the faith and joy that was in Habakkuk's heart, it served in the end as the public prayer and confession of the people of Judah. Habakkuk, in short, functioned in all the ways in which a prophet was to fulfill his office. Through Habakkuk, God himself spoke to his people. In turn, through Habakkuk, his people spoke to God and were led in the way of prayer and confession.

PART TWO

A Dialogue about Evil in the World
(1:2–2:20)

Habakkuk asks about evil in Judah

² How long, O Lord, must I call for help,
 but you do not listen?
Or cry out to you, "Violence!"
 but you do not save?
³ Why do you make me look at injustice?
 Why do you tolerate wrong?
Destruction and violence are before me;
 there is strife, and conflict abounds.
⁴ Therefore the law is paralyzed,
 and justice never prevails.
The wicked hem in the righteous,
 so that justice is perverted.

From the conditions in Judah that Habakkuk describes in these verses, it sounds as though he is writing after the death of Josiah. Josiah was one of the few godly kings of Judah. He conducted a religious reform that included destroying the idol shrines, repairing the temple, and cleansing it courts of the corrupt religious practices of the day. His work didn't last long or go very deep, however, After his death in 609 B.C., his son Jehoiakim came to the throne, and Jehoiakim had none of his father's redeeming qualities. He was an irreconcilable enemy of Habakkuk's contemporary, Jeremiah. It is hard to believe that he was any friendlier to Habakkuk and the group of believers whom Habakkuk served. It seems that the godless attitudes and wicked behavior which were present in the royal house filtered down to lesser officials and, finally, to the people themselves. It is this condition in society that Habakkuk was concerned about.

The prophet's dialogue with God begins with Habakkuk complaining that he has been praying to God for a long time to stop the violence and injustice in Judah, but God has not been listening. Upset that wickedness, strife, and oppression were rampant in Judah while God seemingly did nothing, he cries out, "How long, O Lord, must I call for help, but you do not listen? Or cry out to you, 'Violence!' but you do not save?"

This is not the only time that such a cry from the lips of God's people is recorded in Scripture. The apostle John reports that he saw the souls of those who had been killed for their faithful witness to God's Word. He heard those martyrs calling out in a loud voice, "How long, Sovereign Lord, holy and true, until you judge the inhabitants of the earth and avenge our blood?" (Revelation 6:10).

Neither Habakkuk nor the saints in John's vision spoke these words in a mean-spirited manner. They were not thirsting for vengeance for wrongs the wicked had done to them. After all, the Lord tells his own to love their enemies and willingly turn the other cheek when wronged. Rather, their questions simply ask the Lord when he is going to defend his honor, act justly against the wicked in the way his holiness demands, and deliver his saints in the way he had promised. God himself, after all, gave us this self-description at Mount Sinai as he handed down the law: "I, the Lord your God, am a jealous God, punishing the children for the sin of the fathers to the third and fourth generation of those who hate me" (Exodus 20:5). And even though he told Moses on the mountain that he was "slow to anger" (34:6), he also said that he "does not leave the guilty unpunished" (verse 7). Habakkuk knew what the Lord had said about himself, and so he cries out, How long, O Lord, will I cry for justice and deliverance, and receive no response from you?

Habakkuk asks a second question: Why, O Lord, do you tolerate wickedness in the first place? Again, Habakkuk is not the only one, or even the first one, to put this concern into words. In his suffering, righteous Job had raised the issue: "Why do the wicked live on, growing old and increasing in power? They spend their years in prosperity and go down to the grave in peace" (21:7,13; see also the rest of chapter 21). The psalmist Asaph also confessed that he actually envied the prosperity of the wicked. He wondered, "How long will the enemy mock you, O God? Will the foe revile your name forever? Why do you hold back your hand, your right hand? Take it from the folds of your garment and destroy them!" (Psalm 74:10,11; see also the entire psalm).

Both Asaph and Habakkuk wonder why the Lord has his hands in his pockets, why he takes no action against those who willfully revile him and ignore his will. How, they would ask, can he permit the haughty, wicked person to slap him in the face and dare him to respond, and then make the godly view such behavior or, worse, become victims of it themselves?

What is it that Habakkuk sees that causes him such dismay and prods him to ask such daring questions of the Lord? As this keen observer of his times strolls down the streets of Jerusalem and looks around at the society of his day, he sees "violence" and "injustice" rear their ugly heads on every hand—whether in the hovels of the poor, the palatial homes of the rich, or the shops and booths that line the streets of the business section of the city.

"Violence" describes the immoral or even criminal behavior evident on all levels of Jerusalem society under Jehoiakim: murder, robbery, theft, fraud, embezzlement, rape, adultery, and other flagrant violations of God's moral law. These are sins that flow out of godless minds and unregenerate hearts. They destroy the lives of individuals and ruin the fabric of society. They look very much like the things that fill our society today, do they not?

"Injustice" is the inability or unwillingness of society to react against and punish the "violence" it finds in its midst. Habakkuk observes that the courts are corrupt, that the processes of justice have broken down. Justice is perverted to favor the wicked intentions of the godless, and the godly who play by the rules are taken advantage of. The wicked escape punishment, and the godly find that justice eludes them, or they are ridiculed or persecuted because they refuse to condone evil but rather call for its condemnation and punishment.

The way Habakkuk pictures the law in his society is memorable: "The law is paralyzed." A paralyzed person cannot walk or move his hands; he can't work or defend himself if attacked. So likewise is the law in an immoral society. The law has become ineffective, easy to circumvent, so crippled that "justice never prevails." There is no agreement on what is right or wrong. There is no willingness to effectively punish those who break laws. As a result, the law ceases to function. It becomes unable to dispense proper justice.

An immoral society is a lawless society. Where the Ten Commandments have become a dead letter, the breakdown of law and order in society is the inevitable result. This is what Habakkuk saw all around him, and he wondered why a just God did not act. Why did God tolerate this? Why didn't he save his people and deliver them from the wicked men who were hemming them in? Why had he ever let things get so bad in the first place?

The Lord responds that the Babylonians will punish Judah

> 5 "Look at the nations and watch—
> and be utterly amazed.
> For I am going to do something in your days
> that you would not believe,
> even if you were told.

There is no formal introduction for the Lord's response to Habakkuk's complaint. The prophet here does not begin with "Thus says the Lord," or, as he will later in chapter 2, "Then the Lord replied" (verse 2). Actually, the only reason we know that these verses are not a continuation of Habakkuk's complaint is that they don't make a great deal of sense if we attribute them to Habakkuk. They speak of things which he simply would not be able to do. And they are so phrased that they can only be the thoughts and intentions of him who controls all the affairs of history—in other words, God himself.

How Habakkuk received these words of the Lord, we don't know. It might have been in a dream or a vision. That's how the Lord ordinarily communicated with his prophets. What we do know for sure is that Habakkuk received these words as he "received" the rest of his book (1:1), that is, they were revealed to him by the Lord, probably shortly after Habakkuk lodged his first complaint.

Although it can't be detected in English, the first word of this verse, "Look," is a plural verb in Hebrew. As such, it indicates that the Lord is speaking not only to Habakkuk, but also to the people on whose behalf the prophet had spoken to him. As he speaks, the Lord directs their attention to the world stage: "Look at the nations and watch." He invites them to contemplate the real-life human drama that was in the process of being acted out there—something they would be "utterly amazed" at, something they "would not believe."

Notice that he does not just say, "Watch how the affairs of world history are going to turn out." He says, "*I am* going to *do* something" among the nations "in your days." Contrary to Habakkuk's complaint, God was not inactive. He was not just standing by. He was about to do something, to step in, to intervene, and he was going to do it quickly, "in your days," within the lifetime of Habakkuk's generation.

They were to "look at" and "watch" the events occurring among the "nations" of the world, for he would show himself to be the Lord of heaven and earth, the one who plans and directs how the events of history develop and turn out. Habakkuk and the people of Judah were to realize that nations arise because the Lord raises them up. Nations fall because he decrees their destruction. Nations suffer ruin as the agents of God's wrath carry out those decrees, whose fulfillment God has entrusted to them.

These history lessons, these truths, offer solid and substantial reasons for the wicked to be "utterly amazed," to stand in awe of the Lord, for he can direct his judgment against them too at any time. These truths also provide clear-cut warnings to the wicked, warnings intended to rouse them to repentance before it is too late and God's full-fledged wrath falls upon them.

These truths further serve as a magnificent comfort to the people of God. Things may look bad for the church on earth at times, but the Lord never loses control. Day after day, century after century, millennium after millennium, he directs world events for the good of his people. The group Habakkuk speaks for would come to realize this when they saw events develop exactly as the Lord had said they would.

Interestingly enough, the apostle Paul quotes Habakkuk 1:5 as he is preaching in the synagogue of Antioch in Pisidia: "Look, you scoffers, wonder and perish, for I am going to do something in your days that you would never believe, even if someone told you" (Acts 13:41). In beginning the quote as he does, Paul leaves us with the impression that the Lord was primarily directing his words to the scoffers in Habakkuk's Jerusalem, to the very people whom Habakkuk had designated as "the wicked" in the initial verses of his book. That is possible. There really is only a difference of a single Hebrew letter between the phrases "you scoffers" and "at the nations."

The Lord, however, was not interested in just giving Habakkuk a history lesson, nor was he interested in just making the point that he controlled history. No, there was another lesson to be taught here: the fact that the Lord often used the nations of the world to punish or discipline his people. A hundred years earlier—when wicked King Ahaz of Judah refused to trust in the Lord and believe God's promises to deliver his people—Isaiah prophesied that the Lord would use a foreign power to punish the faithlessness of Judah: "The LORD will bring on you and on your people and on the house of your father a time unlike any since Ephraim broke away from Judah—he will bring the king of Assyria" (7:17). Now, in Habakkuk's day, the Lord was about to do something similar. He would raise another "rod of [his] anger" (Isaiah 10:5) to carry out his punishment on the wicked society of Habakkuk's time, and that rod of the

Lord's anger would come from a most unlikely source. Habakkuk understood these words as the Lord's answer to his complaint.

> ⁶ I am raising up the Babylonians,
>   that ruthless and impetuous people,
> who sweep across the whole earth
>   to seize dwelling places not their own.
> ⁷ They are a feared and dreaded people;
>   they are a law to themselves
>   and promote their own honor.
> ⁸ Their horses are swifter than leopards,
>   fiercer than wolves at dusk.
> Their cavalry gallops headlong;
>   their horsemen come from afar.
> They fly like a vulture swooping to devour;
> ⁹   they all come bent on violence.
> Their hordes advance like a desert wind
>   and gather prisoners like sand.
> ¹⁰ They deride kings
>   and scoff at rulers.
> They laugh at all fortified cities;
>   they build earthen ramps and capture them.
> ¹¹ Then they sweep past like the wind and go on—
>   guilty men, whose own strength is their god."

"I am raising up the Babylonians," the Lord says, revealing what action he would take—namely, sending the Babylonians as the rod of his anger and the instrument of his divine justice. They would be the tools he would use to do the terrible work he had just talked about in verse 5. He describes this as an utterly amazing event—an event so amazing that people would not believe when they were told about it. Their response would be, "You're crazy! That could never happen!"

It was not that Habakkuk or the other people of Judah had never heard of the Babylonians. In fact, it was a Chaldean king ruling in Babylon, by the name of Merodach-

Baladan, who a century earlier had sent ambassadors to King Hezekiah, congratulating him on his recovery from a serious illness.

If we have Habakkuk placed right in history, then Babylon at this time was an independent nation, or kingdom. Its ruler was Nabopolassar, a one-time Chaldean chieftain, who had participated in destroying the Assyrian capital of Nineveh and presently was the undisputed ruler of the Tigris and Euphrates river valleys. The amazing thing was that the Lord was going to use this nation as a rod of discipline for Judah. At this time it didn't seem likely that they would ever be strong enough to extend their power as far as Judah.

The Chaldeans initially were a group of tribes from southern Mesopotamia, each under the leadership of its own chieftain. They moved down into southern Babylon about the middle of the second millennium B.C. and settled near the head of the Persian Gulf. There they managed to maintain a certain amount of independence from whatever force or group happened to be the ruling authority in the area at the time.

When the Assyrians conquered Babylon, reports about the Chaldeans begin to appear in the annals of the Assyrian kings. Nearly every year the Assyrian armies were forced to march into southern Babylon and quash a new rebellion the Chaldean tribes had initiated. Because the Chaldeans refused to submit to the authority of the Assyrians and constantly fought to resist them, they were labeled "anti-Assyrian"—even though they would have resisted *any* force that tried to control them.

Several times when Assyrian authority was weak in Babylon and there was no other strong regional authority, the Chaldeans not only achieved independence for themselves, they also marched to Babylon and seized control of lower Mesopotamia. This is what happened late in the eighth century when Merodach-Baladan sought the support of Hezekiah as an anti-Assyrian ally. The Assyrians reasserted their authority in Babylon, however, and Merodach-Baladan was driven out.

The second time that the Chaldeans asserted themselves in Babylon, the results were more enduring. Nabopolassar, Nebuchadnezzar's father, took the throne of Babylon for himself in 626 B.C. and declared Babylon to be independent of its Assyrian overlords. This time Assyria was too weak to do anything about it, and Nabopolassar became Babylon's new king. This was the beginning of the Chaldean, or New Babylonian, Empire. Fourteen years later, in 612 B.C., Nabopolassar joined forces with the Medes in destroying Nineveh.

After Nineveh was destroyed, the Medes withdrew to the east and left the area of Mesopotamia to the Chaldean Babylonians. A short time later, the Egyptians marched north through Canaan and Syria to the west banks of the Euphrates River to make sure that the Babylonians had no thoughts of crossing the river and extending their power to the west as the Assyrians had done. For about seven years the Euphrates River remained the boundary between the area under the influence of the Babylonians, to the east, and the area under the influence of the Egyptians, to the west. This was probably the situation in Habakkuk's time, and there was no reason for him to suppose that the situation would change anytime soon.

The Lord had his own plans, however—plans no one could have possibly discovered if the Lord had not revealed them to Habakkuk. The Lord says that he would bring the Babylonians right into the land of Judah and the streets of Jerusalem. The first step in this direction, probably several years after Habakkuk wrote, took place in 605 B.C. when Nebuchadnezzar, the general of the Babylonian forces, fought against the Egyptians at Carchemish, in Syria. The Egyptians were decisively defeated and were forced to retreat to their own country. Now the entire eastern coast of the Mediterranean Sea lay open to the Chaldeans. For the first time it became quite evident that they might become a scourge on the backs of the people of Judah.

In fact, shortly after the battle of Carchemish, Nebuchadnezzar, who by this time had replaced his late father as king of Babylon, marched into Syria and Canaan. His purpose was to impress the kings of the area, including Josiah's son Jehoiakim, with his power so that they would not resist his decrees and would willingly pay tribute to him. When Nebuchadnezzar appeared before the gates of Jerusalem in that summer of 605 B.C., Jehoiakim did pay tribute and profess loyalty to him. Nebuchadnezzar also took hostages from the cream of Judean society, to make sure that Jehoiakim didn't change his mind. Daniel was one of those hostages. The Lord's disciplining of his people through the Babylonians had begun.

From the Lord's own description of the people he would raise up to chastise Judah, the thought of what his discipline would entail was not pleasant to contemplate. The Babylonians are described as a "ruthless and impetuous" nation, "a feared and dreaded people." Already in their homeland in southern Babylon they had displayed a warlike quality, and as soon as they ascended to power and began their march of nearly two decades to world domination, their true nature became painfully obvious. After helping the Medes to defeat Assyria, they established a ruthless empire of their own, continuing the Assyrian tradition of terrorizing, looting, and taxing weaker kingdoms of the ancient Near East. If any of the smaller kingdoms of the area, including Judah, had hoped that the Babylonians would provide relief from the cruel aggression of the Assyrians, they were sadly mistaken. Habakkuk portrays the Babylonians as sweeping "across the whole earth," seizing homes and lands and "dwelling places not their own," places they had not controlled before—and never resting until their goal was reached. What made the Chaldeans so formidable was the speed with which their armies traveled and the ferocity with which they attacked. This they had learned from the Assyrians. Isaiah said of the Assyrians, "Here they come, swiftly and speedily! Not one of them grows tired or stumbles, not one slumbers or sleeps; not a belt is loosened at the waist, not a sandal thong is broken. Their arrows are sharp, all their bows are strung; their horses' hoofs seem like flint, their chariot wheels like a whirlwind" (5:26-28). It must have been a frightening sight when the Assyrians came as Isaiah described. Now the Babylonians would do the same.

Babylon's cavalry is compared to three predators whose speed and power bring violent death to their prey. "Their horses are swifter than leopards, fiercer than wolves" who hide during the day and attack "at dusk"—at night. Distance is no obstacle to them as "their horsemen [speedily] come from afar." Like the "vulture" they swoop down with unbelievable speed to devour their prey, to satisfy their lust for slaughter. Habakkuk's description is intended to make the people of Judah picture the Babylonian cavalry overrunning their country, looting, raping, killing, and spreading fear and panic throughout their nation. Everyone in that vast Babylonian army ("they all") comes "bent on violence." The rumor of their frightfulness precedes them and weakens their victims' will to resist before they arrive in person.

Babylonian cavalryman

What a picture of an irresistible force the Babylonians presented. Stopping the advance of such "hordes" of men was as futile as trying to stop the hot scorching "desert wind." They scooped up "prisoners" and collected them for deportation to Babylon just as the wind off the desert swept up innumerable bits of sand. The Babylonians were so intent on capturing their objectives that they would "deride kings and scoff at rulers" and "laugh at all fortified cities" that stood in their way. Nothing would stop them, much less slow them down. They would lay siege to a city and bring it to its knees and then "sweep past like the wind and go on" to their next conquest. One faith sustained them— they always trusted in their own power, firmly believing they could do whatever they wanted to do. Kings of the smaller kingdoms would try in vain to defend themselves and stop the advance of the Babylonians.

But nothing would stop these Babylonians—not natural barriers, like the Euphrates; not armies, even large ones like that of Egypt; not city walls, even strong ones like those that surrounded Jerusalem. All would fall before this powerful enemy. No one could resist them. The revelation God gave Habakkuk was a frightening one for the people of Judah. Doom and destruction lay ahead for them at the hands of these "feared and dreaded people."

The people of Judah were being punished for their lawlessness. They had refused to bow before the standard of God's law. Now they would be overrun by a people who would be "a law to themselves." If the people of Judah wanted to experience lawlessness, they need only wait until the Babylonians came. In their self-sufficiency and arrogance the Babylonians were not going to allow any set of rules and restrictions to keep them from doing what they wanted to do, to keep them from promoting "their own

honor." For them there was no higher law, no higher power
to whom they were ready to defer. "I am the master of my
fate; I am the captain of my soul" might well have been the
motto by which they lived. Ultimately, the only law they followed was that might makes right. No force of moral
authority or conscience would turn these marauders from
the ruin and destruction they intended.

This knowledge of the Babylonians' character, even
before they arrived, must have made Habakkuk wonder
why the Lord chose them as his instrument to punish his
people. Habakkuk describes their spiritual condition as
"guilty men, whose own strength is their god." The
Chaldeans would have scoffed at the idea that the Lord was
using them to discipline his people. Their attitude was like
that of the Assyrians, whom Isaiah describes as saying, "By
the strength of my hand I have done this, and by my wisdom, because I have understanding. I removed the boundaries of nations, I plundered their treasures; like a mighty
one I subdued their kings" (10:13).

For men like Nebuchadnezzar, the idea that the God
of a small, insignificant nation like Judah was Lord of all
the earth who was controlling their destiny would be just
too ridiculous to contemplate. Habakkuk says that the
god of the Babylonians was their own strength. That is
what they worshiped and gloried in. In that pride, however, was the seed of their eventual collapse. Because of
it, they were guilty in God's eyes, and the Lord cannot
and will not tolerate such arrogance. And add to that
the fact that they were still morally responsible for what
they did, even as they were carrying out the task God
had entrusted to them to be the rod of his anger against
his people.

Habakkuk asks about evil among the Babylonians

¹² O LORD, are you not from everlasting?
  My God, my Holy One, we will not die.
 O LORD, you have appointed them to execute judgment;
  O Rock, you have ordained them to punish.
¹³ Your eyes are too pure to look on evil;
  you cannot tolerate wrong.
 Why then do you tolerate the treacherous?
 Why are you silent while the wicked
  swallow up those more righteous than themselves?
¹⁴ You have made men like fish in the sea,
  like sea creatures that have no ruler.
¹⁵ The wicked foe pulls all of them up with hooks,
  he catches them in his net,
 he gathers them up in his dragnet;
  and so he rejoices and is glad.
¹⁶ Therefore he sacrifices to his net
  and burns incense to his dragnet,
 for by his net he lives in luxury
  and enjoys the choicest food.
¹⁷ Is he to keep on emptying his net,
  destroying nations without mercy?

Habakkuk had his answer. But the Lord's answer that he was going to use the fierce, bitterly cruel nation of Babylon as the instrument of his punishment upon Judah must have stunned Habakkuk. The question to be asked here, however, is, When did Habakkuk speak a second time? Did he object right away, as soon as he had digested the full implications of what the Lord had said, or did he wait a while? Some commentators feel that the prophet waited quite a while. They think that this complain of Habakkuk comes after the Chaldeans have invaded the land and Habakkuk has firsthand knowledge of what these marauders are like. This certainly could be the case. If it is so, then this little book was written over a period of time, perhaps as long as several years. It may just be, however, that Habakkuk knows of the Chaldeans from secondhand information, or perhaps from knowledge that he gained from visiting the area where Babylon was located. As is always the case with Habakkuk, trying to add substance to what we know about his life is merely an exercise in speculation. One thing is true, however—Habakkuk does appreciate the devastating aspect of what the Lord has revealed to him. He knows what the Babylonians are like.

But Habakkuk's second address does not begin with a complaint. It starts with a confession. The Lord is the eternal God who controls all things. Habakkuk acknowledges that the invasion of the Babylonians would occur because the Lord had marked his people for judgment. It was a just sentence the Lord was passing on his people. They had earned his condemnation and wrath. The reason that this foreign invader would come was not that the Lord had lost control of the situation, nor had the gods of Babylon defeated the God of Israel, as the heathen of the area might have thought. No, the Babylonians would come because the Lord had prepared them. He had called them for this purpose, and he was using them to accomplish his objectives. Of this the prophet had no doubt.

In verse 12 the NIV translates the second line in this manner: "My God, my Holy One, we will not die." There are many other translations which read, "you will not die." The reason for this difference is to be found in the Hebrew Bible as it was handed down to us by those who copied and preserved the text. Those people are called "Masoretes," meaning "preservers." The Masoretes felt that in certain places earlier scribes had deliberately changed the text for a variety of reasons, one being that the text said something about God that offended them. The Masoretes claimed that this verse originally read, "you will not die," but that the scribes changed the words to "we will not die" because somehow the statement " you will not die" implied that God could die—even though the statement says just the opposite. Whether or not this change actually happened for the reason stated, the Masoretes marked the text here as such in the copies they made of Habakkuk. Translators who follow the Masoretic note will put "you will not die" into their translations. Others who ignore the note and simply use what is found in the text will use the sentence "we will not die." Either one would make sense. Saying that God will not die confesses that it is the eternal God who is controlling the affairs of the world. Saying that "we" will not die would be the prophet's way of affirming that Judah's messianic hope would be fulfilled in spite of the harsh discipline they were enduring.

Habakkuk follows this confession with another affirmation. He says of the Lord, "Your eyes are too pure to look on evil; you cannot tolerate wrong." This certainly is not a statement that is unique to Habakkuk, as though he had a view of the Lord's holiness which was more severe than that of any other inspired writer. Habakkuk was saying nothing different from what David had confessed about the Lord: "You are not a God who takes pleasure in evil; with you the wicked cannot dwell. The arrogant cannot stand in your presence; you hate all who do wrong. You destroy those who tell lies; bloodthirsty and deceitful men the LORD abhors" (Psalm 5:4-6). Saint Paul said something similar hundreds of years later, when he was moved by the Spirit to say, "The wrath of God is being revealed from heaven against all the godlessness and wickedness of men" (Romans 1:18).

Now comes Habakkuk's second question: "Your eyes are too pure to look on evil; you cannot tolerate wrong.

Why then do you tolerate the treacherous? Why are you silent while the wicked swallow up those more righteous than themselves?" Habakkuk did not deny that the people of Judah deserved judgment. He was troubled, however, by the fact that the Babylonians were worse than the people of Judah. Judah ignored God's law, but the Babylonians refused to acknowledge any law but their own. Judah was wicked, but the Babylonians were worse. Shouldn't the Lord's instrument of judgment display something of the Lord's own purity and righteousness?

Furthermore, the Lord's rod was chastening indiscriminately. The righteous in Judah, and there were some, were suffering along with the wicked. Where is the justice in that? Habakkuk feels that God's cure is worse than the disease. Once again Habakkuk was experiencing a mystery which the Lord has not chosen to reveal: how he as a righteous God is ruling in a wicked world. If the oppression by the Babylonians was already in progress, then the cry of the prophet is all the more sharp and intense as he experiences the heavy hand of the Babylonians personally or as he views that hand coming down on those for whom he is speaking.

The prophet Isaiah once used the picture of a child gathering eggs to illustrate the way the king of Assyria plundered the nations he conquered. He has the Assyrian say, "As one reaches into a nest, so my hand reached for the wealth of the nations; as men gather abandoned eggs, so I gathered all the countries; not one flapped a wing, or opened its mouth to chirp" (10:14). Habakkuk uses the picture of a fisherman catching fish to portray the greed and appetite which drove the Babylonians to plunder the way they did. Like the nations that the Babylonians devastated, fish are helpless. They cannot avoid being taken. They are swept away indiscriminately. The net of the Babylonians sweeping through the area simply catches up all nations, including Judah.

Furthermore, like all invading armies, the Babylonians had an eye for the best. They ravished the land and its people, taking the choicest of foods, the best of the people, the costliest of possessions. What they didn't want, they destroyed. What a heavy hand the Lord was bringing against his people. How long would the Lord's anger burn? When would his mercy return?

Probably the most galling thing for a prophet who is interested in the Lord's glory and honor is the fact that after the Chaldeans had conquered Judah, they would not give any praise or honor to the Lord, even though he was the one who gave his people over into their hands. Where does their praise go? Habakkuk says, "He sacrifices to his net and burns incense to his dragnet." The Babylonians credit their weapons—in other words, their own military strength and prowess—for their success. How can the Lord tolerate such idolatry and arrogance?

2 I will stand at my watch
  and station myself on the ramparts;
I will look to see what he will say to me,
  and what answer I am to give to this complaint.

This verse really belongs to chapter 1. It describes the course of action the prophet is determined to take now that he has made his second complaint. Once more he looks to God for an answer. Like a watchman standing on the walls of Jerusalem, alert and waiting for a messenger to come bearing news, he looks out to see or hear what God wants to communicate to him.

The picture of the prophet as a watchman is a familiar one in the Old Testament. At the Lord's direction, the prophet Isaiah once stood as a watchman on Jerusalem's walls, waiting for the news that Babylon had fallen (see Isaiah 21:6-9). God also addressed Ezekiel, his prophet to the exiles in Babylon, as his "watchman." As God's watchman, he received messages from the Lord—in Ezekiel's case, warning messages that God was getting ready to punish the wickedness of his nation. Ezekiel, in turn, sounded the alarm to the people God had entrusted to his care. Jeremiah 6:17 draws the same picture: the prophets the Lord sent are portrayed as watchmen.

The picture is a fitting one. The watchman had to be alert and constantly on his guard. The enemy might appear when he least expected it. Then again a messenger might come with important news, and he had to be ready to receive it. He also had to be patient. If the news that the city was waiting for was delayed and did not come as expected, the watchman still had to stay alert—to watch for the messenger and be ready to communicate the news to the rest of the city the minute the messenger came.

Habakkuk says that he will take up his post, "stand at [his] watch," and wait patiently for the Lord's message. The fact that Habakkuk says that he is waiting for God's answer indicates that the complaint was not his alone, but that the remnant of believers in Judah were waiting for God's answer to be communicated to them as well. The answer that the Lord would give to Habakkuk was one which he, in turn, would give to that remnant.

The Lord responds that the Babylonian evil also will be punished

²**Then the LORD replied:**

> **"Write down the revelation**
> **and make it plain on tablets**
> **so that a herald may run with it.**

> ³ **For the revelation awaits an appointed time;**
>   **it speaks of the end**
>   **and will not prove false.**
> **Though it linger, wait for it;**
>   **it will certainly come and will not delay.**

For the only time in his book, Habakkuk says here that the Lord spoke to him. We do not know how he chose to communicate with Habakkuk. We also do not know how long Habakkuk had to wait for the Lord's answer. While many think that Habakkuk's second complaint was written before Babylon had invaded the land, some feel that the answer waited until the Babylonians came. The reason they feel this way is that the promised relief from Babylon's oppression, which fills the rest of this chapter and the next, seems to fit better at a time when the Babylonians were already a problem for Judah.

Habakkuk voiced his complaint and then confidently waited for the Lord to respond. The Lord did not disappoint his prophet. In answering him, the Lord first tells Habakkuk to "write down" whatever he was receiving in the form of this divine vision (NIV translates this as "revelation"). *Vision* is a technical term for the prophecy or message that the Lord caused Habakkuk to see or hear.

The rest of the directions from the Lord in this verse are not easy to understand. He tells Habakkuk to "make it [the prophecy or message] plain on tablets." Some commentators think that Habakkuk is being instructed to write down the vision in such clear language that no one would misunderstand what he had received. Then anyone who reads the message can run and tell others what he has read. The NIV calls such a person—one who takes a message and runs with it to proclaim it to other people—a "herald."

Others take the Lord's instructions to mean that Habakkuk was to write out the message God gave him in

115

such large, highly visible letters that the words could be read by any person, even one who was running or hurrying by. The "tablets" on which Habakkuk was to write in such a scenario would be placards or posters which could be erected in prominent public places where many could easily read the display. Today we would probably put them on billboards. This interpretation seems to have merit. At any rate, while the specifics of Habakkuk's instructions are difficult to understand, the general thrust of the directions is clear: God wants this message to get out; he wants others to hear or read it; he wants it to have the broadest possible audience.

Then in verse 3, the Lord goes on to talk about certain characteristics of visions and revelations—characteristics which apply not only to Habakkuk's vision but to any vision or revelation a prophet might receive from the Lord. The Lord wants his people to know about these characteristic elements of prophecy. If God's people don't know these truths, then they'll lose hope and will despair when they face oppressors like the Babylonians. There are four such characteristics of prophecies received through visions that will nurture the faith of God's people:

> 1. <u>Prophecy is for an appointed time.</u> "The revelation awaits" means either that this is the way the Lord deals with his people before the time of fulfillment comes, or that prophecy always has a set time of fulfillment that it refers to, even if that time is known only to the Lord. To put it another way, there is an appointed time for the prophecy's fulfillment, a time determined and fixed by the Lord.

> 2. <u>Prophecy cannot wait for (literally, "pants for") its fulfillment to come.</u> This refers, no doubt, to the longing of God's Old Testament

people to see the fulfillment of prophecy, as Saint Peter reveals: "Concerning this salvation, the prophets, who spoke of the grace that was to come to you, searched intently and with the greatest care, trying to find out the time and circumstances to which the Spirit of Christ in them was pointing when he predicted the sufferings of Christ and the glories that would follow" (1 Peter 1:10,11).

3. Prophecy from the Lord proclaims only that which will truly take place in the future. Prophecy from the Lord is never an end in itself. It is always dependable and is a sure foundation for the believer's confidence.

4. Though fulfillment may not come immediately, it will not fail to come at precisely the time that the Lord has set for it.

It is most important that children of faith in all ages understand and take these characteristics of prophecy to heart. These are foundational truths that support the faith of God's people of all times. They are as important for Christians to know and cling to today as they were for the people of Habakkuk's time.

> [4] "See, he is puffed up;
>   his desires are not upright—
>   but the righteous will live by his faith—
> [5] indeed, wine betrays him;
>   he is arrogant and never at rest.
> Because he is as greedy as the grave
>   and like death is never satisfied,
> he gathers to himself all the nations
>   and takes captive all the peoples.

The Lord draws a contrast here between the arrogant unbelief of the Babylonians and the trust which dwells in the hearts of God's prophet and God's people. Both the Lord and Habakkuk have spoken about the pride of the Babylonians previously. The Lord referred to them as "guilty men, whose own strength is their god" (1:11). Habakkuk echoed this sentiment when he said, "[The wicked foe] sacrifices to his net and burns incense to his dragnet" (1:16). In other words, the Babylonians had supreme confidence in their military prowess and especially in their military muscle and might. They pointed to their weapons—the hook and dragnet of the previous chapter—and took pride in how well they had crafted them and how professionally they could employ them.

One can just visualize Babylonian officers and officials strutting through the streets of Jerusalem, thumping their chests, and raising the same impudent cry the Assyrians had in Zephaniah's day: "I am, and there is none besides me" (Zephaniah 2:15). Put that quote of these proud and cocky men alongside one from the God of all creation, history, and existence, who said of himself, "I am the LORD, and there is no other; apart from me there is no God" (Isaiah 45:5). Clearly, the Babylonians, in living out their suffocating pride, had made an idol out of their own strength. Worse yet, in their hearts they felt that they could replace God on his throne. What arrogance! God's assessment of their attitude and character stands: "[their] desires are not upright." (This line could also be translated as "I am not satisfied with him." That is the way the author of Hebrews understood the passage [10:38]. Then this line is not calling the attitude and behavior of the Babylonians wicked but rather is expressing the Lord's displeasure with that behavior.)

This attitude of faith in earthly power is hardly unique to the ancient Babylonians. The Assyrians, as noted previously, entertained similar thoughts. Centuries earlier, Egypt's pharaoh had displayed the same attitude when he said to Moses and Aaron, "Who is the LORD, that I should obey him and let Israel go? I do not know the LORD and I will not let Israel go" (Exodus 5:2). Centuries later it would be the dominant attitude of the Persians, the Greeks, the Romans, and the other conquering nations that followed in their footsteps. More recently, during World War II, it was the attitude of the Germans and Japanese. And it was the attitude the Soviet Union expressed until it collapsed and self-destructed in the later part of the 20th century. Unfortunately, it is also the attitude of the United States—presently the only surviving world superpower—as it flexes its military muscle throughout the world.

Finally, it is the attitude of every sinner ever born into the world. For sinful man, life centers on and revolves around himself. To ignore his Creator and rebel against God's will is his sovereign right—or so he claims. He stands accountable to no one—but himself. He attributes his success to the fact that he is a self-made man—a man who deserves the credit for achieving whatever he has accomplished in life and for fulfilling whatever goals he set for himself. Sound familiar? What arrogance! "His desires are not upright." He—like his Babylonian counterpart of a different time and place—will be condemned.

In sharp contrast to the arrogant, puffed-up, boastfully self-reliant Babylonian, the Lord now places the righteous man, the man of faith. He says, "But the righteous will live by his faith." (Note: This translation is better than the footnote alternative in the NIV, which translates "faith" as *faithfulness.* Although the Hebrew word often means "to act in a faithful or loyal way," the focus here is not on *doing* but on *depending upon* the Lord to act faithfully in accord with his promises.) Faith is holding firm to the God who can be trusted, even though it can't always understand his ways. Faith believes the visions and revelations God gives to his prophets, trusts in God's promises, and, in the face of trouble, difficulty, and calamity, finds its assurance there.

Actually, what the Lord says could be read as "But the righteous by faith will live." The question is where "by faith" is to be placed—with "the righteous" or with "will live"? Is God speaking of those who are "righteous by faith," or is he describing those who "live by their faith"? It seems that both meanings are to be included in the sentence. Perhaps that is why the Lord phrased the sentence the way he did.

Saint Paul takes the sentence in the first sense when he quotes this passage in Romans 1:17 and Galatians 3:11. There he says that a person who is righteous by faith will live. True righteousness before God comes when a person believes in or clings to the righteousness that Jesus Christ has earned for us. When a person receives that righteousness by faith, that believer is able to stand before a holy God and be told: "You are declared just, free of all guilt before me. I have accepted the perfect obedience and the atoning death of my Son on your behalf. You may live with me now and throughout eternity."

The writer to the Hebrews quotes the Lord's words in the other sense. He says, "My righteous one will live by faith" (Hebrews 10:38). He means to say that the child of God, the one who is righteous through Christ, will live his life by faith—that is, trusting that the Lord will never leave or forsake him. Believers can be sure that the Lord will be faithful to his promises to love and care for them. The writer to the Hebrews used this passage to encourage his readers to endure whatever future persecution might confront them with the firm confidence that the Lord would always be at their side. They were to understand that in every circumstance the Lord would be with them, supplying their needs and protecting them. Therefore, the righteous will live by faith.

In Habakkuk, the Lord is using these words in the same sense as the writer to the Hebrews did. God's people—facing a future of harsh discipline from the Lord at the hands of the Babylonians—would live their lives trusting in the promises of deliverance that the Lord had made through Habakkuk and the other Old Testament prophets. In the Lord's own good time their enemies would be punished for their arrogance and be removed from the scene. "Look for the end, the fulfillment of the prophecy, and patiently wait for it," the Lord was telling his people. "Know that I will not fail you, no matter how powerful and invincible your oppressors seem to be. Live your lives with an unfailing confidence in me and my faithfulness."

This sentence, "The righteous will live by his faith," forms the theme of Habakkuk's book. It's *the* truth which Habakkuk—and the Lord through Habakkuk—wants to live and dwell in the hearts of the faithful in Judah. Whether they were facing the wicked unbelievers in their own society or the haughty Babylonians, the believers were to know and believe that God, their faithful God, would deliver them exactly as he had promised.

The fact that this passage is quoted so often in the New Testament indicates that God wants these words to live and dwell in the hearts of his people today as well. Christians—who are righteous by faith in Christ's perfect life of obedience to his Father's will and in his all-atoning death for sin—will live their lives trusting in the Lord and the promises he has made to them. As they confront an unfriendly, unbelieving world, they will confess with Paul, "If God is for us, who can be against us? He who did not spare his own Son, but gave him up for us all—how will he not also, along with him, graciously give us all things?" (Romans 8:31,32). They will look to the future and the end of their life on this earth with trust in the words of Jesus, "I am the resurrection and the life. He who believes in me will live, even though he dies; and whoever lives and believes in me will never die" (John 11:25,26). Yes, the righteous by faith will live!

Now the Lord returns to the arrogant, puffed-up Babylonians, adding even more details to their characterization. He says, "Indeed, wine betrays him." Heavy drinking, drunkenness, and alcoholism afflicted the Babylonian army—as it has numerous others down through the centuries. The consequence? The Babylonian's addiction to drink would play a major role in their ultimate ruin.

At the same time, the expression is also being used metaphorically. The Lord, in using this word, is also speaking of a different kind of wine, one that is equally destructive: the intoxicating wine of pride, arrogance, and self-glorification. It makes good sense to also understand it this way, since the Lord speaks about arrogance and its effects in the rest of the verse.

According to the Lord, arrogance manifests itself in greed. "Because I am everything, I want everything. Because I am everything, I have the right to take anything I want"—such was the attitude of the Babylonians. Their greed was insatiable. They were "arrogant," ambitious, "never at rest," never content, "greedy as the grave" and, like death, "never satisfied." Death and the grave await everyone—expecting all, they won't "turn away" anyone, so to speak. Likewise Babylon—never content, never satisfied, lusting to have all people in its grasp and subject to it—was marching through the Middle East, gathering "to himself all the nations" and taking "captive all the peoples," and wanting still more.

Wine can be a heady intoxicant. It can boost one's ego, make one boastful, and lead one to crave even more, but wine can also boomerang on a person, and the drinker can wind up like a dead man on the floor. Wine can make him an object of ridicule and disgust, and so it was to be with the Babylonians. They too were to be disciplined by the Lord—with a discipline that would mirror what they had done to others. Alcoholism, for example, if unattended, eventually destroys the alcoholic. So the Lord would see to it that the Babylonians, drunk with their own pride, would eventually self-destruct. They carried within themselves the seeds of their own destruction. When that destruction fell upon them, it would not be simply a natural phenomenon; it would be the judgment of the Lord, Israel's Savior-God.

> **⁶"Will not all of them taunt him with ridicule and scorn, saying,**
>
> > **" 'Woe to him who piles up stolen goods**
> > **and makes himself wealthy by extortion!**
> > **How long must this go on?'**
> > **⁷ Will not your debtors suddenly arise?**
> > **Will they not wake up and make you tremble?**
> > **Then you will become their victim.**
> > **⁸ Because you have plundered many nations,**
> > **the peoples who are left will plunder you.**
> > **For you have shed man's blood;**
> > **you have destroyed lands and cities and everyone**
> > **in them.**

After describing the typical Babylonian as a man of intemperance, pride, and greed (verse 5), the prophet begins a series of five woes in which he announces the judgment of

God upon the Babylonians. Each woe describes a certain sinful characteristic or trait of the Babylonians.

In the concluding verses of this chapter, the Lord finishes his answer to Habakkuk's complaint by speaking directly to Babylon about its greedy and imperialistic ways and characteristics. He says that the greedy arrogance, the insatiable lust for conquest, that lay behind the empire's desire to grow and enrich itself at the expense of others would come back to haunt it. In conquering and despoiling the many nations it had, Babylon had made a great many enemies. So when the city and its empire fell, those nations would get back at their conqueror. They would feel no pity for Babylon but would rather heap scorn and ridicule on her with the taunt-song that follows. The song consists of five verses, each beginning with or at least including "Woe to him who . . ." Each one condemns Babylon for its greed and bloodthirstiness. Each one indicates that there would be a certain poetic justice in the punishment that the Lord would inflict upon Babylon.

The fact that the Lord includes such a taunt-song in his answer to Habakkuk has led some to question whether such an attitude can be harmonized with the Lord's own words which declare that he takes no pleasure in the death of the wicked and that he loves all people. That other heathen nations might be filled with hatred toward Babylon and seek revenge we can understand, but the Lord wanted his people to love its enemies, did he not? Why then would he teach them such a song?

The answer involves two very important considerations. First of all, Babylon's arrogance and the way it expressed itself was in reality an attack upon the Lord himself and upon his claim to be the absolute ruler of the affairs of all nations. Babylon used its empire-building conquests not to serve the Lord as an instrument in his punishing hand but to seek and enhance its own glory. Second, the time of the Lord's grace and mercy finally comes to an end for any and every nation. Assyria, one of the world's true superpowers before the rise of the Babylonians, had had its time of grace. The Lord had even sent the prophet Jonah to Nineveh, Assyria's capital city, to call its people to repentance. For a time the king of Nineveh even led his people in repentance, but Nineveh later rejected God's mercy, and God sent the prophet Nahum to sing a song of scorn over the arrogant, unrepentant city and to proclaim its doom.

A similar fate awaited Babylon. The prophet Daniel would labor there under King Nebuchadnezzar, and in various ways he would bring the heathen king to recognize who really was Lord of all. But as the Lord's patience and long-suffering came to an end for Nineveh, so it would for Babylon as well. An arrogant, greedy empire-builder like Babylon could also expect to hear the Lord laughing in scorn over its attempts to exalt itself above him and over its oppressive treatment of his people. For all nations that exalt themselves against God and seek to hinder the coming of his kingdom can expect the Lord to act as the psalmist says he will: "Why do the nations conspire and the peoples plot in vain? The kings of the earth take their stand and the rulers gather together against the LORD and against his Anointed One. 'Let us break their chains,' they say, 'and throw off their fetters.' The One enthroned in heaven laughs; the Lord scoffs at them. Then he rebukes them in his anger and terrifies them in his wrath, saying, 'I have installed my King on Zion, my holy hill'" (Psalm 2:1-6).

The first woe condemns Babylon for accumulating wealth for itself while building its empire. Such ill-gotten wealth, such getting rich at the expense of those whom they had oppressed and extorted, will not last long. Habakkuk uses the picture of a debtor building up debt by borrowing more and more. Eventually, the creditors will come and demand what is owed them. So Babylon should view its wealth as goods which it "borrowed" by force, by twisting the arms, so to speak, of those whom it conquered. One day all those nations whom they had oppressed and plundered would "suddenly arise" and turn the tables on them. They would one day return with the same force and demand that the Babylonians pay up. That Babylon did its debt-building at the expense of many human lives and the destruction of much property is condemned as well.

> ⁹ **"Woe to him who builds his realm by unjust gain**
> **to set his nest on high,**
> **to escape the clutches of ruin!**
> ¹⁰ **You have plotted the ruin of many peoples,**
> **shaming your own house and forfeiting your life.**
> ¹¹ **The stones of the wall will cry out,**
> **and the beams of the woodwork will echo it.**

The second woe condemns the violence Babylon had used in collecting its unjust gain regardless of how much ruin and devastation it had caused. The city was aware that it had made many enemies with its conquests and looting and plundering. One way of remedying the situation would have been to grant justice to these nations. Instead, Babylon chose to isolate itself and make itself unapproachable. Habakkuk compares its attempts to make its present dynasty secure and put itself out of reach from its enemies to those of an eagle building its nest in an inaccessible place where no enemy could reach it. Perhaps Babylon could isolate itself behind its walls and close its ears to the clamoring for justice which came from the cities and countries it had ruined, but it couldn't escape the cry of truth. If its victims failed to raise their voices to condemn Babylon, then the very stones and wooden beams it had plundered from others and used to construct the houses and palaces and temples of Babylon would have to cry out, "Our rightful owners were robbed and murdered to bring us here! Woe to the city of blood!"

> ¹² **"Woe to him who builds a city with bloodshed**
> **and establishes a town by crime!**
> ¹³ **Has not the LORD Almighty determined**
> **that the people's labor is only fuel for the fire,**
> **that the nations exhaust themselves for nothing?**
> ¹⁴ **For the earth will be filled with the knowledge of the glory**
> **of the LORD,**
> **as the waters cover the sea.**

In Nebuchadnezzar's time, the city of Babylon was one of the seven wonders of the ancient world. With its hanging gardens, "mountain-high" walls, and magnificent buildings— Nebuchadnezzar's palace being the outstanding example— Babylon surpassed all other cities as a monument to what human ingenuity can accomplish. Daniel indicates that Babylon was built for man's glory when he quotes Nebuchadnezzar as saying, "Is not this the great Babylon I have built as the royal residence, by my mighty power and for the glory of my majesty?" (Daniel 4:30).

In the third woe, however, the Lord condemns the bloodthirsty cruelty that the Babylon Empire used to gain the wealth and procure the slave labor that had built its beautiful capital. Its building program was carried out at the price of the sweat and blood of the conquered nations. The mortar and nails that held the buildings together were the blood of the conquered nations whom Babylon slaughtered.

Such building projects might last if the one in control were not the Lord Almighty. In his world, the Lord punishes such criminal activity; he pronounces a sentence of doom upon it: "Has not the LORD Almighty determined that the people's labor is only fuel for the fire, that the nations exhaust themselves for nothing?" The punishment may not happen right away. The Lord usually doesn't strike down evildoers with a bolt of lightning at the very moment they are committing their atrocities, but eventually the moment of doom will come. The seventh wonder of the world, with all its magnificent buildings and everything that had been used to build and create it, would go up in smoke and leave behind nothing but dust and ashes. Once again, the Lord's punishment of Babylon would mirror what the Babylonians had done to other nations. They had torn down what belonged to others to build up their own. Now they would be torn down and destroyed.

The Lord then establishes a general principle. The empires and kingdoms and works of human beings all eventually come to nothing. Men spend their lives working to build things for their glory or to enhance their reputation, only to have the fruits of their labor destroyed by the conquerors who follow them. One world power follows and destroys its predecessor. That's what history records, and history will continue to repeat itself in the same vein until the very end—so says the Lord.

But the knowledge of the Lord's glory will last forever. Isaiah says the same thing in almost the same words: "The earth will be full of the knowledge of the LORD, as the waters cover the sea" (11:9). "The glory of the LORD" is the sum total of what he is as he has revealed it to mankind. In the New Testament, the apostle Paul says, "God, who said, 'Let light shine out of darkness,' made his light shine in our hearts to give us the light of the knowledge of the glory of God in the face of Christ" (2 Corinthians 4:6). If the full knowledge of the glory of God can be known only in the face of Christ, then the greatest fulfillment of Isaiah's and Habakkuk's words is found in the spread of the gospel of Jesus Christ throughout the world—in building a kingdom that will not lie in ruins someday, but will last for an eternity.

> ¹⁵ "Woe to him who gives drink to his neighbors,
>   pouring it from the wineskin till they are drunk,
>   so that he can gaze on their naked bodies.
> ¹⁶ You will be filled with shame instead of glory.
>   Now it is your turn! Drink and be exposed!
> The cup from the LORD's right hand is coming around to you,
>   and disgrace will cover your glory.
> ¹⁷ The violence you have done to Lebanon will overwhelm you,
>   and your destruction of animals will terrify you.
> For you have shed man's blood;
>   you have destroyed lands and cities and everyone in them.

The fourth woe condemns the moral depravity with which Babylon subdued the nations it had conquered. Forcing a person to drink from a cup of wine until he's drunk is a figure the prophets used to denote the way conquerors like Babylon humiliated the people they ruled over. Staring lewdly at their nakedness depicts the way Babylon used these nations to satisfy its own lusts and appetites. Obviously, being forced to walk naked before the leering eyes and scoffing mouths of the those who conquered them was a very humiliating experience for those so oppressed.

Now, the Lord says, it was Babylon's turn. All the humiliation it had heaped upon others would now be heaped upon it. The Lord would make Babylon drink the cup of humiliation. In its defeat it would reel and stagger like a drunk. For sinning and causing others to sin, they would soon be drinking from the cup of God's wrath, and the result for them would be even greater shame and disgrace than what they had heaped upon other nations.

Other nations might be the agents, but Babylon's downfall would not be a case of simple human revenge. The Lord himself would deal out justice and judgment to this violent and immoral city. Now it was their "turn" to "drink and be exposed." The cup of wrath "from the LORD's right hand" was about to be handed to them. And how they deserved to be condemned for what they had done, for the mass destruction of human life and property they had caused: "For you have shed man's blood; you have destroyed lands and cities and everyone in them." Their shameful abuse of God's creation for their own selfish purposes—"the destruction of animals" and the "violence" they had "done to Lebanon" and places like it by ravaging the trees and forests and other resources—were also part of the reason they would now have to drink from that cup of wrath. What they had done to others would now come around to them, only in much greater measure.

> [18] **"Of what value is an idol, since a man has carved it?**
> > **Or an image that teaches lies?**
> > **For he who makes it trusts in his own creation;**
> > **he makes idols that cannot speak.**
> [19] **Woe to him who says to wood, 'Come to life!'**
> > **Or to lifeless stone, 'Wake up!'**
> > **Can it give guidance?**
> > **It is covered with gold and silver;**
> > **there is no breath in it.**
> [20] **But the LORD is in his holy temple;**
> > **let all the earth be silent before him."**

The form of the fifth, and final, woe is a little different from the others. God's pronouncement of woe appears in the middle of the stanza, not at the beginning. More important than the form, however, is the subject matter of this final woe, for it is the most serious indictment the Lord brings against Babylon. The other curses are bad enough—they spell out the particulars of Babylon's self-glorification and its inhumane treatment of its neighbors. This final woe accuses the city and its people of denying their natural knowledge of God, the creator of all things and the ruler of the world. They had substituted a worship of created things for the worship of the Creator himself. That's idolatry. The apostle Paul says it this way: "Although they knew God, they neither glorified him as God nor gave thanks to him, but their thinking became futile and their foolish hearts were darkened. Although they claimed to be wise, they became fools and exchanged the glory of the immortal God for images made to look like mortal man and birds and animals and reptiles" (Romans 1:21-23).

The main thrust of the Lord's accusation is that the Babylonians worshiped objects their hands had made. They put their trust in their "own creation"—these dumb, lifeless objects made of wood and stone that "cannot speak." They called on them to "come to life" and help them. They prayed to them and begged them for help. And while many of these idols were beautiful and costly objects, they never responded, they never answered. They couldn't. They were dumb, helpless, useless objects, objects with no breath animating them. To worship such a god is pure folly. (For the most stunning condemnation of the foolishness of idol worship, read Isaiah 44:9-20.)

Now idol-worshipers from Babylon, or anywhere else for that matter, would probably argue that they weren't worshiping the idol—that it was just a symbol or representation of their god. The way the Lord argues here, however, indicates that popular heathen piety did, indeed, see the idol as the god. The people brought offerings to feed it and clothe it. They carried it in parades as an object of adoration. They brought their prayers to it. They fell down in adoration before it. For all practical purposes, they were worshiping wood and stone.

In the end, however, even the so-called gods behind these idols were merely personifications of the forces of nature, much the way people of our age view Mother

Nature. These too were created things. Whether the heathen worshiped things God created or objects their hands had made or creations of their own imaginations, the end result is the same. They were worshiping created things in place of the Creator and were allowing these idols to usurp God's rightful place in their lives. God forbids that in the very first commandment.

So where should the attention of Babylon's worship have been directed? The Babylonians would have been surprised at the answer. The Lord of heaven and earth had made his home in the temple in Jerusalem, in the lowly, unimportant country of Judah. Although he has made all things and the entire universe cannot contain him, he, in his mercy and compassion, has deigned to make his earthly dwelling among men. There he would let his voice be heard. There he would hear the prayers of his people—those he sought to make his own from throughout the world.

At the temple's dedication, King Solomon made it clear that the Lord's dwelling in Jerusalem was for the benefit of *all* people. He prayed, "As for the foreigner who does not belong to your people Israel but has come from a distant land because of your name . . . when he comes and prays toward this temple, then hear from heaven, your dwelling place, and do whatever the foreigner asks of you, so that all the peoples of the earth may know your name and fear you, as do your own people Israel, and may know that this house I have built bears your Name" (1 Kings 8:41-43). There the Lord was present because he chose to be. There the people of the world should stand in awed silence, as is fitting behavior for sinful creatures before the Lord of all.

Here the Lord reassured his disturbed prophet: "Habakkuk, I see Babylon's sinful behavior. Rather than complaining that I am doing nothing about it, remain silent, and wait for me to carry out my righteous judgment."

PART THREE

A Psalm of Faith in the Lord's Justice and Saving Power
(3:1-19)

A call for the Lord to deliver as he has in the past

3 A prayer of Habakkuk the prophet. On *shigionoth.*

Once again, Habakkuk is designated as a prophet. Inasmuch as there are some indications in this chapter that the psalm it contains was used in public settings, it would appear that Habakkuk here is fulfilling that aspect of the prophetic office where he speaks *to* God *for* the people (see page 93 for an extended commentary on the prophetic office). What Habakkuk said here in pouring out the personal convictions and hopes and beliefs that were in his heart, the people later made their own and used as a confession of their faith. The prophet not only spoke for God's people. He taught God's people to speak for themselves, offering them his own divinely inspired words for their use if they wished to do so. Perhaps such a use of his psalm is what Habakkuk intended all along.

Nobody knows for sure what "shigionoth" signifies. There does seem to be considerable agreement, however, that it refers to some musical direction or melody according to which this psalm was to be sung. The fact that such directions appear here and at the end of the chapter and that the threefold "Selah" occurs throughout the psalm indicates that the psalm was intended for and used in public worship. Since it expresses the kind of patient, trusting faith which the Lord said resides in the heart of the believer (2:3,4), it forms a fitting conclusion to the book.

Although this chapter is different form-wise from anything else in Habakkuk and would seem to be more at home in the book of Psalms, content-wise it's the expected result of God's Spirit working in the human heart. Therefore, those who had a faith similar to that of Habakkuk's dwelling in their hearts might well have been drawn to use this psalm as an expression of their confidence in the Lord.

It has been suggested that the psalm was used in Israel as a song of victory when the Babylonian Empire was finally overthrown some 70 years later. It may also have served as a song of trust in the Lord whenever his people were faced with any kind of oppression and danger. Whatever its specific use, Habakkuk's personal expression of faith in this beautiful hymn of praise became a treasure of all the Old Testament people of God.

> ² LORD, I have heard of your fame;
>   I stand in awe of your deeds, O LORD.
> Renew them in our day,
>   in our time make them known;
>   in wrath remember mercy.

In 2 Timothy 1:5, Saint Paul says of his young coworker, "I have been reminded of your sincere faith, which first lived in your grandmother Lois and in your mother Eunice and, I am persuaded, now lives in you also." Timothy had heard of the mighty, saving acts of God because the members of his family had taught him. How Habakkuk heard of the Lord's fame and learned of his deeds, we don't know. There is no record. But if the members of Habakkuk's family were of the same God-fearing mold that Timothy's mother and grandmother were, then someone in his family must have taken the time and made the effort to teach Habakkuk all about what he is about to confess.

It has been said that the Christian church is always just one generation away from absolute ignorance about the Savior-God. This is a valid observation because no one is born with a knowledge of or confidence in the gracious love of God and the salvation of sinners that he has accomplished in Jesus Christ. What Moses told the Israelites about God's laws—"Teach them to your children" (Deuteronomy 11:19)—is the God-given assignment of every new generation. Whether it's Habakkuk's generation or ours, whether it's the revealed law of God or his marvelous act of rescue in Jesus Christ, children will not know, will not be able to confess as Habakkuk did, if they haven't been taught. There is no more solemn or necessary responsibility laid upon parents and the church of any age than to teach the next generation what the Lord has done for them and expects of them.

Recalling the record of the Lord's past works of deliverance fills the prophet with hope. What God did in the past, he can do again. Habakkuk now pleads with God to intervene on the people's behalf as he had in the past. He prays, "Renew them in our day." In chapter 2 the Lord said that prophecy longs for the day of its fulfillment. Habakkuk pleads with the Lord to "make [your deeds] known" in "our time," to bring that fulfillment about in his day. He begs the Lord to coat his wrath with mercy and, by doing so, to save his people. The Sons of Korah, some of Israel's premier psalmists, expressed a similar longing when they sang, "We have heard with our ears, O God; our fathers have told us what you did in their days, in days long ago. But now you have rejected and humbled us; . . . Awake, O Lord! Why do you sleep? . . . Rise up and help us; redeem us because of your unfailing love" (Psalm 44:1,9,23,26).

> **³ God came from Teman,**
> **the Holy One from Mount Paran.**   **Selah**
> **His glory covered the heavens**
> **and his praise filled the earth.**
> **⁴ His splendor was like the sunrise;**
> **rays flashed from his hand,**
> **where his power was hidden.**
> **⁵ Plague went before him;**
> **pestilence followed his steps.**
> **⁶ He stood, and shook the earth;**
> **he looked, and made the nations tremble.**
> **The ancient mountains crumbled**
> **and the age-old hills collapsed.**
> **His ways are eternal.**
> **⁷ I saw the tents of Cushan in distress,**
> **the dwellings of Midian in anguish.**

Having prayed that the Lord might bring swift judgment and justice on the Babylonians, the prophet now looks into the future and sees God coming to judge the Babylonians and to deliver and rescue his people in much the same way that he came to Israel in the exodus and in the Mount Sinai region.

In the Old Testament, when the Lord was pictured as coming to the rescue of his people, he is often portrayed as coming from the south. This is perfectly natural because the Lord appeared to Moses and the children of Israel at Mount Sinai, which lies to the south of Canaan. The wilderness area where the Lord cared for his people for 40 years also lies to the south. It was that area of the land which, to the pious Israelite, represented the place of God's saving deeds. Moses spoke in just such terms when he wished to hold the Savior-God before Israel's eyes. "He said: 'The LORD came from Sinai and dawned over them from Seir; he shone forth from Mount Paran. He came with myriads of holy ones from the south, from his mountain slopes. Surely it is you who love the people; all the holy ones are in your hand. At your feet they all bow down, and from you receive instruction, the law that Moses gave us, the possession of the assembly of Jacob'" (Deuteronomy 33:2-4).

Teman is a district of Edom that lay to the southeast of Canaan. Edom was the country that the Israelites had to bypass as they traveled to the spot east of the Jordan River from which they would enter the Promised Land. Mount Paran is associated with the wilderness of Paran, which lay in the Sinai Peninsula, south of Canaan.

Speaking the way he does, Habakkuk is picturing Israel's covenant-God coming to rescue his people in their hour of desperate need. He describes an appearance of the "glory" of the Lord. At critical times in the history of his people, God put on visible clothing, as it were—appearing as blinding brightness, flame, cloud, and smoke—to defeat his enemies and deliver his people. In Habakkuk's psalm he appears as a warrior armed for battle. This brilliant imagery describes the theophany, this special appearance of God in which he is majestically and personally carrying out his work of judgment and salvation.

The Lord is pictured in ways that display his power as he comes to deliver his people. That is what the Lord's "glory" is here. When God came, Habakkuk says, his "splendor was like the sunrise"—his glory shone like the light of the sun rising spectacularly in the east. Blinding "rays [of light] flashed from his hand" like lightning bolts. The light of his glory filled heaven and earth. Bright light often is used by God in his appearances to represent his overwhelming glory. When the Lord appeared to Ezekiel to call him as a prophet, Ezekiel says, "I saw that from what appeared to be his waist up he looked like glowing metal, as if full of fire, and that from there down he looked like fire; and brilliant light surrounded him" (Ezekiel 1:27).

Plague and pestilence are pictured as servants of the divine King, standing in his presence, waiting to execute his bidding. In his role as judge and avenger, plague walks before the Lord, and pestilence follows behind. With this imagery Habakkuk wishes to portray the Lord as one who comes in judgment of his enemies in order that he might deliver his people. In the book of Ezekiel, the Lord speaks of his four dreadful judgments: sword, famine, wild beasts, and plague (14:21). Likewise in the Revelation of Saint John, the apostle sees the sword, famine, plague, and wild beasts marching out into the world to bring God's wrath on the abode of sinners. We cannot hear of Plague attending the approaching Savior-God without remembering the plagues by which the Lord delivered his people from slavery and from the heathen pharaoh who refused to acknowledge him.

Seismic activity also is used to represent the Lord's power. Habakkuk speaks of the Lord shaking the earth and causing the mountains to crumble as if they were nothing more than the walls of Jericho. To speak of "age-old hills" and "ancient mountains" as crumbling and collapsing is like saying that the very foundations of the earth were shaken. This is no ordinary earthquake that Habakkuk is describing, not even one with a high number on the Richter scale. This is a convulsing of nature, which is jarred and disturbed as its Creator approaches. The nations also shudder in mortal fear as he comes. His mere glance is enough to make them "tremble."

Such disturbing events in nature are frequently associated in the Old Testament with Israel's march to Mount Sinai and through the wilderness. The psalmist says that the hills skipped like rams and lambs at the Lord's approach. He calls out, "Tremble, O earth, at the presence of the Lord, at the presence of the God of Jacob" (Psalm 114:7).

No wonder nations like Cush and Midian were distressed as the Lord passed by with his people. These groups were desert dwellers living in northern Arabia and eastern Sinai. They were close to the path Israel took during the exodus.

> ⁸ **Were you angry with the rivers, O LORD?**
>   **Was your wrath against the streams?**
> **Did you rage against the sea**
>   **when you rode with your horses**
>   **and your victorious chariots?**
> ⁹ **You uncovered your bow,**
>   **you called for many arrows.**   *Selah*
> **You split the earth with rivers;**
> ¹⁰   **the mountains saw you and writhed.**
> **Torrents of water swept by;**
>   **the deep roared**
>   **and lifted its waves on high.**
> ¹¹ **Sun and moon stood still in the heavens**
>   **at the glint of your flying arrows,**
>   **at the lightning of your flashing spear.**
> ¹² **In wrath you strode through the earth**
>   **and in anger you threshed the nations.**

Habakkuk now illustrates the energetic action that the Lord expended when he rescued his ancient people. The imagery may seem excessive and unfamiliar to us, but it is language that prophets who preceded Habakkuk used to describe the Lord's work. The imagery comes from the myths of Canaan and other nations that surrounded Israel. This doesn't mean that the prophets believed these myths or that they felt their readers did. It was simply a poetic way of speaking about what the true God really did, in language that was familiar from other literature. The situation is similar today when people say, "Mother Nature certainly showed her power and determination with the thunderstorms and tornadoes that struck us today." Christians might rephrase this, substituting "the Lord" for "Mother Nature" to testify to who really is behind the awesome events that happen in nature.

In Canaanite mythology, Rahab was a monster of chaos and disorder. Accompanying her was a dragon called Lotan, whom the Bible gives the name Leviathan. The heathen god whom the Canaanites credited with creating the earth is pictured as slaying this chaos monster and her pet dragon. The writer of the book of Job uses this imagery to give credit to the Lord for creating the world. In a spirit of joy and praise, Job proclaims, "By his power [the Lord] churned up the sea; by his wisdom he cut Rahab to pieces. By his breath the skies became fair; his hand pierced the gliding serpent" (26:12,13).

Isaiah used similar language to proclaim the Lord's manifestation of his power over the sea when dividing the Red Sea so that Israel could pass through to begin the exodus. He says, "Was it not you who cut Rahab [referring here to Egypt] to pieces, who pierced that monster through?" (Isaiah 51:9). In this context Isaiah is calling on the Lord to act at the present time on behalf of his people as he did in the past, for in the words that begin the verse Isaiah says, "Awake, awake! Clothe yourself with strength, O arm of the Lord; awake, as in days gone by, as in generations of old." What Isaiah did, asking the Lord to act on behalf of his people as he had in the past, is exactly what Habakkuk was doing. Habakkuk used language that emphasized this theme. His first readers would relate to what he was speaking about, not only by what he said but also by the imagery he used to say it.

The Lord is pictured as a mighty warrior who unleashes the full force of his weapons against his enemies. Nature bows before the Creator who has given it order. If this mighty God wishes to interfere with the laws of nature in order for him to accomplish the deliverance of his people, then so be it. He can move mountains and change watercourses. Even the sun and moon will stand still if the Lord so wills that he might complete his people's victory over their enemies. We are reminded of what the Lord did in Joshua's time during the conquest of Canaan. "Joshua said to the LORD in the presence of Israel: 'O sun, stand still over Gibeon, O moon, over the Valley of Aijalon.' So the sun stood still, and the moon stopped, till the nation avenged itself on its enemies, as it is written in the Book of Jashar. The sun stopped in the middle of the sky and delayed going down about a full day" (Joshua 10:12,13). In order to give Joshua's army more time to defeat the enemy and to make sure that the enemy army would not be able to escape under cover of darkness, God lengthened the time of sunlight. What normally takes 24 hours took 48. Habakkuk prays that the Lord would act in his day the way he did for Joshua.

The impact of the Lord's power on nature is not incidental, of course. The sun and moon didn't stand still just so the Lord could show off his power. He did it so that he could deliver his nation from her enemies. That is what Habakkuk wants as well. In order to save Israel, the Lord has shown his willingness to thresh the nations (always a picture of judgment and destruction). Their history bears witness to that fact. Now Habakkuk wants that threshing machine to run through the land once more, in order that Babylon might be destroyed and Israel might be delivered from oppression and death.

¹³ **You came out to deliver your people,**
    to save your anointed one.
You crushed the leader of the land of wickedness,
    you stripped him from head to foot.   *Selah*
¹⁴ **With his own spear you pierced his head**
    when his warriors stormed out to scatter us,
gloating as though about to devour
    the wretched who were in hiding.
¹⁵ **You trampled the sea with your horses,**
    churning the great waters.

The real purpose of the Lord's coming in power and glory is now stated. When the Lord came, he came "to deliver [his chosen] people." He wished "to save [his] anointed one," no doubt the king who stood as a representative of the entire nation. Again, the language at the end of verse 13 and into verse 14 reminds us of the mythological battles of the gods against monsters. In these myths the sea often represents chaos and disorder. The Lord is pictured as subduing the sea by trampling it with his horse's hooves and churning its waters.

By now Habakkuk's point is clear even to us who are not familiar with these myths. The Lord has come with power, power great enough to give order to creation, in order to deliver his beloved people. In the trampling of the sea Habakkuk may have in mind the way the Lord divided the Red Sea under Moses' rod. That was a very vivid way that the Lord showed his ability to control and direct nature for the good of his own. Habakkuk's references to the leader of the land of wickedness who is stripped naked, and the slaying of the gloating one who was about to devour the hiding ones may also remind us of Pharaoh and his willingness to use his whole army if necessary to crush Israel. The Lord refused to allow that happen, and he used his almighty power to prevent it. Habakkuk longs for that same power to now come to Judah's aid.

A confession of the Lord's gracious power to save

¹⁶ I heard and my heart pounded,
   my lips quivered at the sound;
decay crept into my bones,
   and my legs trembled.
Yet I will wait patiently for the day of calamity
   to come on the nation invading us.
¹⁷ Though the fig tree does not bud
   and there are no grapes on the vines,
though the olive crop fails
   and the fields produce no food,
though there are no sheep in the pen
   and no cattle in the stalls,
¹⁸ yet I will rejoice in the LORD,
   I will be joyful in God my Savior.

¹⁹ The Sovereign LORD is my strength;
   he makes my feet like the feet of a deer,
   he enables me to go on the heights.

The prophet has ended his majestic hymn in praise of the Lord's saving power. Now he returns to reality. Earlier in his book Habakkuk had questioned the way that the Lord runs the world. He does so no longer. He now knew what lay in the future because the Lord had revealed it to him. God was going to send the terrible scourge of the Babylonian armies, and Judah was going to be sorely oppressed. Poverty and desolation would come to a land that had once flowed with milk and honey.

When Habakkuk spoke these words, the Babylonian onslaught may already have begun. The thought of this unhappy prospect affected his entire body and left him with a feeling of helplessness and terror. His heart was pounding, and his lips were quivering. His legs were shaking, and his whole body felt weak and sick. The immediate future was not pleasant to contemplate, and Habakkuk was not looking forward to it. The closing verses of his prophecy, however, are not a litany of despair. The book of Habakkuk does not end with a whimper, but on a note of triumph.

What an amazing statement comes out of the prophet's mouth. He says, "Yet I will wait patiently for the day of calamity." It is easy, or at least relatively easy, to serve the Lord when everything is going well and his blessings are in evidence everywhere. An attitude of thanksgiving comes to us much more easily when crops are good, the stock market is up, inflation is low, all is well with our families, and peace reigns in the land.

But what happens when those blessings are removed? That is what Habakkuk describes here. Because of the Babylonian devastation of the land, crops will fail and the sheep folds and cattle stalls will be empty. Economic conditions in the country will be so bad that the question might be asked how Judah will even survive. For all outward appearances it seemed the Lord had either forsaken his people or lost control of the situation. That is when the faith of the "righteous," the believing child of God, takes over. The prospects for the future had agitated Habakkuk. His faith in the Lord's promise calmed him and strengthened him. His feet had begun to falter, but now they're swift and sure, like the feet of a deer.

He looked at the severe chastisement that the Lord was bringing on Judah, but he no longer complained, "God, why are you punishing your people by a nation more wicked than they are?" Instead, he lays this beautiful confession before us: "I will rejoice in the LORD, I will be joyful in God my Savior." Whatever strength he needed to face the troublesome times ahead, the Lord, he believed, would provide without fail. The Lord would enable him to skip like a deer rather than plod along in despair. His feet would barely touch the ground, a picture of joy and a carefree spirit.

For the director of music. On my stringed instruments.

Habakkuk's words of faith are words to be remembered and applied. "The righteous by faith will live" is not just a catchy motto. It's a way of life. Habakkuk shows us how that way of life will manifest itself in confession and everyday living, especially during days of despair. These closing words remind us that the people of Judah used Habakkuk's words to bolster their own faith in the unfailing goodness of the Lord. They sang them in the worship services that took place in Jerusalem. They sang them in exile and at hard times, not only during the Babylonian oppression but for generations after, when Babylon was a distant memory and other enemies threatened. Habakkuk's words can be our strength and comfort as well, as the righteous continue to live by their faith.

This is Habakkuk's message to us. God's ways may appear strange to us, even unjust, but if, like Habakkuk, we will let God explain them to us, we too will find cause to rejoice and praise him.

INTRODUCTION TO ZEPHANIAH

Author

Zephaniah is one of those biblical writers about whom we know very little. We don't know where he was born or where he lived. We do know, however, that he called Jerusalem "this place" (1:4) and was familiar with the topography and the various sections of the city. That has led a good number of scholars to assume that he was a citizen of Jerusalem.

Zephaniah does something unique among the prophets. He traces his genealogy back four generations and identifies himself as the great-great-grandson of a man called Hezekiah. It seems rather strange that Zephaniah would carry his genealogy back this far if this Hezekiah wasn't an important individual. Many scholars feel the best candidate for Zephaniah's famous ancestor is King Hezekiah, who ruled over Judah from 727 to 698 B.C. Hezekiah was a man who feared and loved the Lord and served him with great vigor. He wanted his people to love and worship only the true God. So he carried out many religious reforms in Judah. He ordered all the idols in the kingdom to be destroyed. He also repaired and purified the temple and reestablished the Passover celebration. He was one of only two kings of Judah besides David who received the Lord's total approval for the way he ruled.

King Hezekiah also happened to be the great-grandfather of Josiah, the king who ruled while Zephaniah was active. If King Hezekiah is the ancestor referred to here, then

Zephaniah and Josiah were cousins, and both of them viewed Hezekiah as a model disciple of the Lord and looked to him as a man worthy of imitating. We might say that all three of them were kindred spirits—men who longed for the nation of Judah to return to the Lord in faith and life and who were willing to devote their lives to seeing that happen. Zephaniah probably labored between 632 and 622 B.C. and strongly supported his king, as Josiah went about carrying out reforms in Judah.

Wrestling with these historical questions and trying to answer them is an interesting exercise, but in the end it doesn't matter all that much whether King Hezekiah was Zephaniah's great-great-grandfather or not. The divine message is the most important thing, not the messenger and his background. Ultimately, Zephaniah is important because the Word of the Lord came to him.

Date and background

Zephaniah reveals that the Word of the Lord came to him during the reign of Josiah, son of Amon. Josiah ruled in Judah from 640 to 609 B.C. We don't know exactly when or for how long a period of time during those years Zephaniah was active. Looking at the various segments of Josiah's reign may, however, give us a clue. Josiah's reign can be divided into three parts. The first part covers the first seven years of his rule. Josiah came to the throne at the age of eight when his father Amon was assassinated. Amon had continued the pro-Assyrian policies of his father, Manasseh, but as Assyria's power waned in this part of their empire, an anti-Assyrian party came into power in Judah. They soon became dissatisfied with Amon, and when he wouldn't change his policies, they got rid of him. Then they had his young son placed on the throne. Josiah was the king, but the real power behind the throne lay in the hands of these influential anti-Assyrian advisors.

The second segment of Josiah's reign began in 632 B.C., when he was 16. At this time, an important change took place in Josiah's life. Second Chronicles chapter 34 reports that in that year "he began to seek the God of his father David" (verse 3). Perhaps what happened was that Josiah came out from under the influence of his early advisors and began to look to men like the prophet Zephaniah, who, above all, wanted to see the entire nation of Judah return to the Lord. During this time we are told that Josiah "began to purge Judah and Jerusalem of high places, Asherah poles, carved idols and cast images" (verse 3).

The third segment of Josiah's reign began ten years later, in 622 B.C., when he began to repair and purify the temple. During this temple repair project, the high priest found the Book of the Law, which formed the basis for the rest of Josiah's spiritual reforms (2 Kings 22:1–23:30; 2 Chronicles 34:1–35:24). Josiah continued this important work until his untimely death in battle against the Egyptian army in 609 B.C.

The best place to put Zephaniah in this history is perhaps during the second period of Josiah's kingship. That is when godly influences began to have an effect on the king's thoughts and activities and he began to institute his reforms. Zephaniah's prediction that the remains of Baal worship would be wiped out of the land (1:4) would fit in with this time when Josiah was carrying out the first steps of his reformation. Although he may have been active longer than the ten years of Josiah's second period, Zephaniah's relationship to Josiah and what he says seem to fit best in the period between 632 and 622 B.C. This would make him a contemporary of Nahum, Habakkuk, and Jeremiah. In fact,

Zephaniah and Jeremiah may have worked together to support Josiah's work in the same way Haggai and Zechariah worked together after the return from exile to support Zerubbabel's rebuilding of the temple.

Theme and content

It is not difficult to ascertain Zephaniah's theme. He states it for the first time in the seventh verse of the book, "Be silent before the Sovereign LORD, for the day of the LORD is near." Zephaniah is not the first prophet to emphasize the day of the Lord. He follows Joel in this respect. Other prophets also addressed the topic. Isaiah (2:6-22) and Amos (5:18-20) both devoted sections of their prophecies to the day of the Lord, but none have made it the centerpiece of their message as Joel and Zephaniah have.

Both Joel and Zephaniah spoke of the "day of the LORD" in a twofold way: (1) as God's judgments occurring in the midst of history against certain individuals and rebellious nations, and (2) as God's judgment day at the end of the world. In fact, the day of the destruction for any enemy of God that takes place in time, in history—be it the fate of an individual, a group, or an entire nation—is for that party or person the day of the Lord, "the last day," on which the sentence of everlasting rejection and eternal destruction is pronounced and executed. So the Day of the Lord came for Assyria in 612 B.C., when it was destroyed by the Medes and Babylonians. It came for Jerusalem in 586 B.C., when Jerusalem was destroyed by the Babylonians, and it came for the Babylonians, in turn, when they fell in 530 B.C. Such individual "last days," occurring in time, were merely phases and forerunners and warnings announcing the coming of the Lord's final day of judgment upon all the earth.

So both Joel and Zephaniah saw God's judgment as an ongoing process, with the culmination coming on judgment day. Each individual "day of the Lord" was a type or foreshadowing of the greater judgment of the Lord that was to come—the time when the course of human history as we know it on this earth will come to an end. That "day of the LORD" will affect not just one individual or nation but all people, all nations, all creation. For this is God's ultimate and universal day of reckoning, the day when justice is triumphant and evil is swept away.

According to Zephaniah, the day of the Lord is a day of wrath and punishment, a day when God will severely punish the nations. He warns, "The great day of the LORD is near—near and coming quickly. . . . That day will be a day of wrath" (1:14,15). Both the faithless hypocrites among God's people and the unbelieving and idolatrous heathen of the world will have the Lord's anger and unrelenting punishment to look forward to on that day.

At the same time, the day of the Lord will be a day of deliverance and rejoicing for the people of God. Zephaniah assures the children of the Lord who listened to him, "On that day they will say to Jerusalem, 'Do not fear, O Zion; . . . The LORD your God is with you, he is mighty to save'" (3:16,17).

This dual view of the day of the Lord as a day of judgment for some and deliverance for others leads to sharp contrasts in the content of Zephaniah's message. The book itself is a unit. It is not made up of a series of isolated, disconnected prophecies about the day of the Lord. The individual thoughts of the book are tightly woven together into a single piece of cloth. The colors in that cloth, however, vary greatly. Most of Zephaniah's revelation consists of the dark, somber, even terrifying colors of God's law and judgment. The cold and lukewarm among God's chosen people will not be overlooked when the judge of all the earth comes. They will find to their despair that a mere outward connection to the body of believers, without a heart filled with repentance and faith, puts them face-to-face with God's wrath. Those who scoff and assume that the end will never come will be surprised and horrified to find out that God is as true to his threats as he is to his promises. The heathen nations of the world will find that the God whom they ignored is determined to judge and condemn their sins as well.

Interwoven with these colors of despair and judgment, however, are the brilliant and joyful colors of the Lord's gospel of deliverance. The day of the Lord will be a day when that which believers have always clung to will become obvious. Then it will be clear to one and all that the Lord has forgiven sin, because the punishment that sin deserves has been taken away. It will not fall on the heads of God's people. When the Lord takes his people to their eternal home, then it will be compellingly clear and most obvious that he wants to dwell with them, that he delights in his relationship with them, that he rejoices over their presence in his eternal abode. Different as these emphases of judgment and deliverance on the day of the Lord are, Zephaniah does a masterful job of bringing them together into one unified proclamation.

Purpose

Some scholars have pointed out that Zephaniah's message is timeless. The times in which he lived don't have all that much connection with his message—outside of the fact that he draws upon them to provide the imagery and manner of speaking he needs to convey his revelation to his readers. In this way he differs from his contemporaries among the minor prophets. Nahum and Habakkuk, whose prophecies accompany Zephaniah's in this volume of The People's Bible, are very much involved in the events of their times. Nahum looks back at the past, the oppression that the nation of Assyria laid upon Judah, and proclaims that the Lord is about to destroy Nineveh and deliver his people from the Assyrian tyranny. Habakkuk looks into the future. He sees the fierce Babylonian armies entering the land of Judah, and he warns that the Lord is about to use this heathen nation as he had used the Assyrians—to punish the unfaithful and wicked behavior of the people he called his own.

Zephaniah, however, rises above history and his times. Wickedness *is* mentioned in terms of Zephaniah's day—wickedness as it was in Judah and in the nations around Judah, but it could have been the wickedness of any age and the faithlessness that is *always found* in God's church as long as it remains on earth. Enemies are mentioned, and deliverance from them is promised. The identity of these enemies is vague and unimportant, however. They are the enemies of the Lord and of his people of all ages. Such enemies will be destroyed; his people will be delivered eternally.

In this timelessness of Zephaniah's message is found a purpose that is also timeless. We can apply Nahum's and Habakkuk's words to ourselves as we enter the 21st century, but first we must find out what those prophets were saying to the people of their day. Then we can ask, "Out of the specific situations these men of God were dealing with, what general truths apply to us?" Zephaniah, however, speaks directly to us. Yes, it's true that he speaks about the church of God in terms of Old Testament Israel: the wicked world is represented by Judah's neighbors on every side, and deliverance comes to the "Daughter of Zion" (3:14). But once we look beneath the Old Testament clothing Zephaniah's message wears, we find the body of truth that Zephaniah sets forth—a body of truth that is as directly applicable to us as it was to the nation of Judah. Zephaniah's words warn us about sin and comfort us with promises of the Lord's deliverance as directly as the words of Jesus do when he warns and comforts in view of the coming day of judgment, the coming day of the Lord.

Outline

Theme: The day of the Lord is near!

   I. The title (1:1)

  II. The Lord's day is a day of wrath and judgment (1:2–3:8)

     A. All creation will be destroyed (1:2,3)
     B. Judah will be punished (1:4-13)
     C. The whole world will be consumed (1:14–2:3)
     D. The nations will be judged (2:4-15)
     E. Faithless leaders will be condemned (3:1-8)

  III. The Lord's day is a day of deliverance and rejoicing (3:9-20)

     A. The Lord will purify the nation (3:9-13)
     B. The Lord will dwell with his forgiven people (3:14-17)
     C. The Lord will restore his people (3:18-20)

PART ONE

The Title
(1:1)

1 **The word of the LORD that came to Zephaniah son of Cushi, the son of Gedaliah, the son of Amariah, the son of Hezekiah, during the reign of Josiah son of Amon king of Judah:**

The title for Zephaniah's prophecy sets before us both the miraculous and the human element in the inspiration of Scripture. The Lord did not reveal his truth directly to the world. He used agents. Those agents, like Zephaniah, received the word of God in a way we do not understand and are at a loss to explain. The word of the Lord was something separate from them and came from a divine source outside of them, and yet it became an integral part of them. When Zephaniah opened his mouth to speak, it was not the Lord's voice that sounded. When he took up his pen to write, it was not the Lord's hand that moved. Zephaniah's voice spoke, using words that were common to him, and Zephaniah's hand moved, writing words that were normal for him, but when he did so, it was the word of the Lord, not Zephaniah's word, that resulted. Zephaniah spoke with *his* voice, and yet at the same time confidently asserted, "[so] declares the LORD" (1:3). Without presuming to explain the miraculous in some rational manner, Zephaniah simply stated what Peter later described: "Prophecy never had its origin in the will of man, but men spoke from God as they were carried along by the Holy Spirit" (2 Peter 1:21).

How reassuring it is to know that Zephaniah is speaking the Lord's pure truth, word for word, and is not simply speaking his own mind. The prophet is going to say some astounding things. He is going to say that the Lord is about to destroy the entire world. Is he to be believed, or is he just a crackpot, an out-of-control alarmist? His readers need to know. If he is mentally deranged or just angry at the world and everything in it, then to believe him would be the height of folly. But if he is right, then to ignore him could mean being caught unprepared for the most catastrophic event in the history of the universe. Sinners would meet their righteous judge when they were totally unprepared to do so.

Zephaniah is going to say that the Lord has taken away the punishment for sin from his people. Is he right, or is he misrepresenting God? Can those who hear Zephaniah's words really dare to hope that the Lord will not hold their sins against them? Zephaniah assures us that he is not guessing about the warnings and promises coming from his mouth. The word of the Lord came to him. He is the Lord's mouthpiece.

(See the Author and Date and Background sections of the introduction [pages 146 to 149] for details about Zephaniah's ancestry.)

PART TWO

The Lord's Day Is a Day of Wrath and Judgment
(1:2–3:8)

All creation will be destroyed

> ² "I will sweep away everything
> from the face of the earth,"
>
> declares the LORD.
> ³ "I will sweep away both men and animals;
> I will sweep away the birds of the air
> and the fish of the sea.
> The wicked will have only heaps of rubble
> when I cut off man from the face of the earth,"
>
> declares the LORD.

Zephaniah doesn't waste any time. He starts his book out with a sweeping statement, one that puts the reader in absolute shock because of the magnitude of what it says: "I will sweep away [or, bring to an end] everything." A day of reckoning is approaching, says the Lord, a day on which "everything" will be swept away. You can't get more inclusive than that. The entire earth will be swept clean. The landscape will appear like a barren desert—from horizon to horizon, there will be nothing in sight on its sandy surface. It will resemble a floor that an extremely powerful vacuum cleaner has swept clean—without leaving the smallest crumb behind.

The scope of this final judgment matches the scope of creation on the fifth and sixth days of the week of creation, when the Lord populated the earth. Then his omnipotent power was displayed in the wide variety and in the great numbers of the kinds of animals with which he filled the earth. Now that same power will be displayed in reversing creation, as it were—that is, by the removal and destruction of all he created. The scope of this destruction will be more extensive than the destruction at the time of the flood. Then all human beings (except for Noah and his family), together with the animals on the earth and in the sky (except those God saved in the ark to help Noah start a new world), were "blotted out," or destroyed. On the day of judgment there will be no exceptions—only a complete and final sweeping away. Every living creature from the land, sky, and sea—yes, even the fish—will be cut off from the face of the earth and perish on that day. So thorough and unrelenting will be the Lord's destructive hand.

The clause "The wicked will have only heaps of rubble" could just as well read, "The aforementioned creation will all be ruins, together with the wicked." The devastation of nature will be a visible, violent witness to the fact that the Lord will rise up in judgment over the wickedness of the sinner. Jesus states that before judgment day, upheavals in nature, such as earthquakes, will be signs of the times (Matthew 24:6-8) and are to remind us that the day of judgment is just around the corner. Zephaniah ties the massive destruction of creation to judgment day itself. When the Lord in his final judgment cuts man off "from the face of the earth" and condemns the wicked for all eternity, nature itself will be violently disturbed and destroyed.

Why is such a violent witness necessary? In the blindness of sin, the sinner cannot appreciate just how serious his condition is. He mutters and grumbles that God is overreacting to his slight imperfections and protests that he is basically a good person. God reveals to him that in his divine courtroom the situation is far worse than he could ever imagine. And the Lord raises a powerful witness, the destruction of creation, to tell him exactly that. What a sobering thought! Sin is so bad in God's eyes that not only is the sinner threatened with hellfire, but creation itself is brought to the brink of destruction. What a powerful call to repentance before that final day comes.

We also ought to remember that this prophecy of destruction may very well have been given even as the godly King Josiah took the first steps of his reforms in Judah. Commendable as his actions were, no reforms initiated by individuals or human institutions, such as the government, will ever remove the threat of judgment that the Lord casts over the world. This is true no matter how successful such human reforms may be. Human beings cannot reform themselves to the Lord's satisfaction. There can be only one proper response to Zephaniah's revelation of coming judgment: Repent, for the day of the Lord is near.

Judah will be punished

4 "I will stretch out my hand against Judah
and against all who live in Jerusalem.
I will cut off from this place every remnant of Baal,
the names of the pagan and the idolatrous priests—
5 those who bow down on the roofs
to worship the starry host,
those who bow down and swear by the LORD
and who also swear by Molech,
6 those who turn back from following the LORD
and neither seek the LORD nor inquire of him.

The Lord's impending judgment may cover the entire world, but as the apostle Peter says, "It is time for judgment to begin with the family of God" (1 Peter 4:17).

Jesus stated a principle that the divine judge will follow here. Jesus said, "From everyone who has been given much, much will be demanded; and from the one who has been entrusted with much, much more will be asked" (Luke 12:48). From the very beginning, the Lord had blessed and honored the nation of Judah more highly than any other. Even before they were a tribe, their forefather Jacob had declared that Judah would be chief among the 12 tribes. The scepter would not depart from them, and the Messiah, the rest-giver Shiloh, would come from their midst (Genesis 49:8-10).

The Lord chose David from a family of Judah to be the king of his people, and he promised David that in Christ his kingdom would endure forever. The Lord saw to it that his earthly house was built in the city of Jerusalem in the kingdom of Judah. Yes, blessing upon blessing had been bestowed upon Judah. Yet, a close relationship with the Lord and being under the umbrella of his grace does not exempt a person or a nation from divine scrutiny; rather, it increases those occasions. Through the prophet Amos, the Lord told the ancient people of Israel, "You only have I chosen of all the families of the earth; therefore I will punish you for all your sins" (Amos 3:2).

According to Zephaniah there was plenty to condemn in the social, moral, and religious conditions that existed in Jerusalem and Judah in his time. In Jerusalem stood the house of the one true God, the place where God himself had pledged to dwell among his people. But Zephaniah reveals that the city and the country surrounding it were full of idolaters, fence-straddling people involved in impure worship, and people who were indifferent to the Lord. These three groups on whom the Lord's judgment will fall deserve a closer look.

Israelites worship Baal

Gross idolatry was still very much present in the land of Judah. Throughout their history the Israelites could never manage to break away from their love affair with the Canaanite fertility-god Baal. As a nation, Israel had first come into contact with Baal at Peor. This was east of the Jordan River, across from the city of Jericho. Moses had led the Israelites there. It was to be the staging area from which they would mount their invasion of the Promised Land. While they waited there, some of the men "began to indulge in sexual immorality with Moabite women, who invited them to the sacrifices to their gods" (Numbers 25:1). This is how the Israelites first got involved in the immoral fertility rites associated with Baal worship.

What began at Peor continued on and off throughout the period of the judges and the kings. When civil war split the nation of Israel into two kingdoms—Israel and Judah—Baal worship became the official religion of the kingdom of Israel during the time of Ahab and Jezebel. (Baal is the Canaanite god that Elijah put to the test in 1 Kings 18:20-40.) The same thing happened in Judah under Jezebel's daughter, Queen Athaliah. Even when Baal worship was not being promoted by the government, it refused to go away, right up to Zephaniah's time. His contemporary, Jeremiah, complained that Baal shrines were located on every high mountain and under every large tree—the locations of choice for such shrines.

The Lord was never timid in his response to Baal worship, either. At the very outset, at Peor, he sent a plague among the people. During the time of the judges he repeatedly punished the Israelites by handing them over to their enemies. During the period of the monarchy he sent the prophets, who thundered against Israel's infidelity to the Lord. There were times when such expressions of the Lord's displeasure were effective. The prophet Samuel and King David ended the Baal worship of the period of the judges, and godly kings like Hezekiah destroyed Baal shrines and reconsecrated the temple. But the people, at least some of them, continued to be attracted to Baal worship and gave this heathen idol the devotion and thanksgiving that belonged only to the Lord of glory.

The Lord promises that his judgment will fall hard upon Baal worship. Every remnant of it will be destroyed. When he says that the names of the pagan and idolatrous priests will be "cut off," he is asserting that not only won't they practice their heathen rites any longer, but that the very memory of their doing so will be blotted out of the people's minds, so that even their names will no longer be mentioned. (Note: The word that the NIV translates as "pagan" here really is a name for a sub-group of Baal priests. In 2 Kings 23:5 they are designated as the ones who burned incense to the idol. The sense of the Lord's words here is this: "I will do away with the names of the incense burners, yes, with all the priests of that despicable idol Baal.")

What made Baal so alluring to God's people in Old Testament times was the fact that his adherents claimed that he was in control of the forces of nature which Israel depended upon in Canaan. He was the rain god, and in a land of marginal rainfall, Israel needed the rain to come regularly. When it didn't, the threat of drought and famine loomed immediately. Baal also was the god of fertility. He was credited with making animals, fields, and human beings fertile. Without Baal's blessing, your field didn't produce crops, your cow didn't calve, your wife didn't bear children. Hence the many fertility festivals and rites—connected with all sorts of immoral sexual practices—which were carried out in his name. In worshiping Baal, Israel was personifying a force of nature and thereby making the mistake of worshiping the creation instead of the Creator, who alone brought rain and fertility to his people.

Baal worship is long gone. It doesn't threaten to corrupt believers anymore. But whenever God's children place their trust and sense of well-being in bank balances, retirement planning, insurance policies, a sound economy, and medical know-how, the spirit of Baalism survives, and *the Creator's gifts* become the foundation of confidence *rather than the Creator himself.* God's keen eye of justice still identifies these sins within the family of God and threatens them with judgment.

In its idol worship, Judah didn't limit itself just to Baal. Zephaniah also condemns those people who went up on their roofs and worshiped the sun, moon, and stars. Certainly these practices were part of Canaanite paganism along with Baal worship. Ten miles west of Jerusalem was a village called Beth Shemesh (meaning "House [Temple] of the Sun"). Fifteen miles east was Jericho, a city named after the moon—perhaps because of the practice of worshiping the moon there.

However, worshiping the sun and moon as deities was much more common in Assyria and Babylon. Already at the time Abraham left Mesopotamia, his childhood home, the worship of the moon-god, Sin, was very common. In fact, Joshua implies that Abraham's father may have been an adherent of Sin (Joshua 24:2). Now, in Zephaniah's day, Abraham's descendants, the people of Judah, were caught up in the same practices. They may have done so for practical reasons. Such worship may have been the politically correct way of showing their loyalty to their Assyrian overlords, or they may have gotten involved in the religions of these powerful countries because they seemed to work so well for their followers. After all, weren't their countries winners, while Judah was a loser? Whatever the reasons, some people of Judah became devoted to these idols. When Jeremiah condemned the worship of the Queen of Heaven, her followers responded that things went right for them only when they worshiped her (Jeremiah 44:15-18). Today, whenever God's people are moved to believe or do things solely because they are *practical* or because they *work*, rather than because they are *true*, then the same spirit that motivated Judah's idol worshipers remains—and so does the threat of the Lord's judgment.

The second group the Lord condemns are those who tried to be loyal to the Lord and to idols at the same time. This practice is called syncretism. It involves mingling the truth with falsehood. The problem with this practice is that, just as mixing impure water with pure water results in more impure water, so it is the pure worship of the Lord that is corrupted when the practices of idol worship are mixed in with it. Zephaniah talks about an idolatrous compromise some people tried to make. They bowed down and swore allegiance to the Lord, but they also had no qualms about using the name of an idol when they took an oath. In so doing they acknowledged and worshiped both—thus showing their divided loyalties.

The name in Hebrew for the idol mentioned here is *Malcam*. The Hebrew word can be translated as "their king," but it might also be pronounced "Milcom." Milcom was the chief god of the Ammonites. He also went by the name Molech. Molech was a hideous god. Human sacrifices, especially of children, were offered to him in the valley south of Jerusalem. To associate or mix the Lord's name with the name of such an idol or to think that one could have a relationship with both at the same time was an abomination and an insult to the Lord.

Such divided loyalties, unfortunately, are still common in the church today. People announce and confess their devotion to Christ, but at the same time they rely on horoscopes or fortune-tellers to guide them or help determine what the future holds for them. Or they may also mix elements of the occult, like spiritism, into what are otherwise wholesome activities. Such syncretism is as unacceptable to the Lord today as it was in Zephaniah's day.

The final group in Judah that the Lord confronts through Zephaniah might best be labeled as "the indifferent." These people grew up in God-fearing families. They had been taught to trust in the Lord and to serve him, but something happened as they went out on their own. They got caught up in their day-to-day lives and in the world around them. Pretty soon they found that didn't have any time for the Lord—nor were they interested in making time for him. They never actually rejected the Lord in just so many words. They just chose to ignore him. Zephaniah speaks of them as "those who turn back from following the LORD." We would probably call them *backsliders* or *apostates*—people who turn their backs on the Lord after once following him.

The second part of this group is different from the first only in degree. Zephaniah describes them as "[those who] neither seek the LORD nor inquire of him." These people had some outward connection with the Lord. Perhaps they even participated in the temple services once in a while, but the Lord simply played no role in their daily lives. They didn't seek out his Word, nor did they study it or apply it to their lives. They seldom, if ever, sought the Lord in prayer or bothered to thank him for his blessings. At best, he played a marginal role in their lives.

If the description of these people sounds familiar, it is because they still can be found in the church today. In fact, all Christians must confess that—to one degree or another—these sins afflict them as well. The Lord hates the sin of indifference as much as he hates the sin of rejection. The exalted Christ had such sins in mind when he said to the church in Laodicea, "I know your deeds, that you are neither cold nor hot. I wish you were either one or the other! So, because you are lukewarm—neither hot nor cold—I am about to spit you out of my mouth" (Revelation 3:15,16).

Some commentators feel that what Zephaniah is doing here is predicting the reforms that Josiah was going to carry out in Judah within the next few years. A comparison of the reforms enacted by Josiah (2 Kings 23) with the description Zephaniah supplies here certainly shows some similarities—especially in the steps taken to eliminate Baal worship. The Lord's judgment, like Josiah's activities, was meant to serve as a cleansing and purifying of Judah in addition to punishing the wicked in her midst. Josiah's work, however, never accomplished the absolute removal of idolaters, nor did it identify the indifferent and punish them, in the way that Zephaniah speaks of the Lord's judgment here. So it's better here to see Zephaniah using Josiah and his ridding the land of the wicked as imagery for the far greater and complete cleansing of the land at the Lord's hands when he comes to judge the whole earth.

> ⁷ **Be silent before the Sovereign LORD,**
> **for the day of the LORD is near.**
> **The LORD has prepared a sacrifice;**
> **he has consecrated those he has invited.**
> ⁸ **On the day of the LORD's sacrifice**
> **I will punish the princes**
> **and the king's sons**

and all those clad
   in foreign clothes.
⁹ On that day I will punish
   all who avoid stepping on the threshold,
who fill the temple of their gods
   with violence and deceit.

The word Zephaniah uses to command silence is the same as our word "Hush!" It is a strong command, calling for immediate and absolute compliance. The reasons are given. The people of Judah are standing before the Sovereign Lord. He is lord and master of the whole earth; he is God, who has chosen and saved Israel. In his presence the only proper response is silence. This is especially true in view of the fact that the day of the Lord is coming, that the day of the Lord's righteous judgment is near. Certainly this holds out the strongest possible reason for the people of Judah to give up their idolatry and return in true repentance to their Savior-God.

It was necessary for Zephaniah to issue this command. Otherwise, the people who read his words would have responded to them the way most people do when a charge is leveled against them. They become defensive. They claim they are not guilty of the charge, or they insist that the charge against them is not serious—at least not as serious as the accuser says it is. They claim he is being unfair. But to take a stand like that before the Judge of all the earth is worthless. The only way to stand before the Lord, Zephaniah advises his readers, is to stand in silent awe and reverence and repentance. This alone displays the right and proper relationship that is to exist between the Lord of all and his creatures, who have rebelled against him.

To describe the punishment the Lord has in store for his wicked people, Zephaniah uses a striking new picture in verse 7. He speaks of the Lord preparing a sacrifice. The

167

sacrifice spoken of here is the fellowship offering—one of the four blood offerings that were instituted in the Mosaic Law. In making this offering, the worshiper brought an animal to the sanctuary, confessed his sins over the animal's head, and gave it to the priest to be sacrificed. What was different about the fellowship offering was that a portion of the meat from the sacrificial animal was given back to the worshiper. And then that meat was shared with the worshiper's family and friends and other invited guests in a joyous family festival. Their eating part of the sacrificial meat together signified happy fellowship with the Lord and with one another, much as Holy Communion does today, also based on the shedding of blood.

Zephaniah now uses this imagery in a most unexpected way. The Lord is the one who supplies the sacrifice. This sacrifice is the nation of Judah, whose blood will be shed. The "guests" whom the Lord has designated to share in the eating of the sacrifice are the invading troops, probably Babylonians, whom God invites to share in the plundering of Judah. What irony! A sacrifice which normally expressed Israel's covenant relationship with God and which was meant to proclaim forgiveness, joy, and peace now becomes a picture of God's judgment.

This is not the first time a prophet foretold the Lord's calling heathen nations to punish his people. One hundred years earlier, the Lord through Isaiah had said to wicked King Ahaz, "In that day the LORD will whistle for flies from the distant streams of Egypt and for bees from the land of Assyria. They will all come and settle in the steep ravines and in the crevices in the rocks, on all the thornbushes and at all the water holes" (7:18,19). It would happen again in approximately 40 years when the Lord would bring the Babylonians against Judah. This invasion, which resulted in the defeat and exile of Judah, certainly was a preliminary fulfillment of Zephaniah's words from here through verse 13. But we must remember that the ultimate reference of the prophet's words is judgment day, the end of all things. The "day of the LORD" that would overtake Judah at the hands of the Babylonians would be only a foretaste of the final judgment.

The first segment of Judean society to fall under the Lord's judgment is its grandest, the king's relatives. When Zephaniah speaks of the princes and the king's sons, he could be looking into the future, to a day when Josiah's sons, who refused to walk in the footsteps of their God-fearing father, were killed or exiled to foreign lands. He also could be referring to the nobles, state officials, and other members of the extended royal family who enjoyed special privileges in the country. Zephaniah characterizes them as people who dress in foreign clothes. In and of itself, the kind of clothes these people wore was neither right nor wrong. The Lord had laid down very few stipulations concerning clothing in the Mosaic Law. But when he did, it had some-thing to do with the people's relationship with him (for example, see Numbers 15:37-40, where tassels on garments are required to remind the wearers to keep God's command-ments). The point is that wearing foreign styles displayed a certain mindset. It showed that the members of the royal family admired and were influenced by the customs and beliefs they found in the heathen cultures of Assyria, Baby-lon, and Egypt. Perhaps the kind of clothing the godly in Judah wore looked dowdy and hopelessly out of style to them. As such, the clothing these people wore became a sign of the rejection of Israelite ways and of the Lord himself.

American Christians may have some trouble identifying with Zephaniah's concern. They are members of the dominant Western culture, and people of other nations imitate them, rather than the other way around. Still, the general principle is true. No society, including our own, can claim that everything in its culture is good. Certain clothing, harmless in itself, or certain symbols in jewelry or on T-shirts can come to symbolize Christless or godless thoughts and lifestyles. Wearing such things may contradict what Christians say they believe or may blunt their confession of Christ before the world. Under such conditions, things which are otherwise neutral in themselves can become wrong. That the rest of the world is doing something is not an excuse for the Christian to join in. In fact, it may even be a reason for the Christian not to do so.

The references Zephaniah makes in verse 9 were, no doubt, readily understood by the people of his day, but they are something of a mystery to modern readers. The first question that arises is, Who is the prophet condemning here? Is he still speaking of the princes and other officials of the previous verse, or does he have a different segment of society in mind? If it's a new group, then more than likely it's the priests of Judah that are being referred to. Second, the custom Zephaniah is speaking about is uncertain. It's true that the Philistine priests at the temple of Dagon in Ashdod avoided stepping on the threshold of their temple ever since their idol had fallen there before the captive ark of the Lord (1 Samuel 5:1-5), but the verb Zephaniah uses seems to imply more than just "stepping over" something. It speaks more of "jumping" or "leaping" in exuberance and joy. So it may even be that Zephaniah is talking about a totally different heathen custom. Whatever the practice was that Zephaniah had in mind, it was totally unacceptable to the Lord.

Finally, the word translated as "gods" by the NIV can refer to idols or human masters, or it can be a word to describe the Lord. So who are the people being described here? They could be princes who practiced heathen customs before the Lord's temple and who brought offerings they had obtained in some violent or fraudulent way, or they could be priests who did the same thing. They might also be people who served the nobles in Judah, servants or slaves who filled the houses of their masters with ill-gotten gain. Whatever their situation might have been, they are cited as further examples of wickedness in Judah and, as such, come under the Lord's condemnation.

> ¹⁰ "On that day," declares the Lord,
>   "a cry will go up from the Fish Gate,
>   wailing from the New Quarter,
>   and a loud crash from the hills.
> ¹¹ Wail, you who live in the market district;
>   all your merchants will be wiped out,
>   all who trade with silver will be ruined.

To picture the Lord's approaching judgment on Jerusalem, Zephaniah describes the advancement of an enemy army on the city of Jerusalem—invading the city from the north, the direction from which its most feared enemies, Assyria and Babylon, came. The prophecy came true in a preliminary way when the armies of King Nebuchadnezzar of Babylon invaded Jerusalem in 586 B.C. Again we need to remember, however, that Zephaniah, using Old Testament pictures from Judah's experience and history, is also referring to the final judgment of God upon all the wicked—whether they have outward connections with the people of God or not. The last and greatest fulfillment of these words will not take place until judgment day, when the Lord will condemn all the wicked, inside the church and without. That will be the ultimate "day of the Lord."

In the days of Solomon (about 950 B.C.), Jerusalem consisted of the temple mount and a long, narrow tongue of land that extended south from there. Two hundred years later, the city had expanded west across the shallow Central Valley to the southwestern and northwestern hills. Hezekiah enclosed parts of those hills when he extended the walls of Jerusalem. The most vulnerable part of the city lay to the north, where neither hills nor valley separated it from the surrounding landscape.

So Zephaniah pictures the invading army approaching the Fish Gate, located in the northwest portion of Hezekiah's wall. That is where the Israelite watchmen would sound the warning. That is where the inhabitants of Jerusalem would first cry out in pain as they felt the enemy's swords strike home. The New Quarter, or Second Quarter, was the newest housing development in the city. It too was located in the northwest corner, west of the temple, and once the Fish Gate had been breached, it would have been starkly vulnerable. The "hills" may also have been a newly developed area in the city. It too would have been easy pickings for the enemy. The wailing and crashing sounds Zephaniah mentions indicate the terrible human suffering involved in such a ruthless invasion and the destruction of the walls, houses, and buildings that would accompany such an invasion.

The next section of the city Zephaniah mentions was zoned for commerce. Zephaniah calls it "the Mortar," or "the Hollow" (NIV: "the market district"). Most commentators assume that it refers to the Central Valley, or Hollow, that ran north and south through the city between the old settlements to the east and the newly constructed ones to the west. This was the business district where the merchants plied their trades and bankers weighed out gold and silver.

This would probably be the next section of the city to fall to the invading army. The verbs Zephaniah uses here paint interesting pictures. (Note: The word that the NIV translates as "be wiped out" could better be translated as "be silenced.") They suggest a situation like this: At first there would just be the normal commotion and noise from the hustle and bustle taking place in the marketplace. That would be followed by the even louder wailing and howling and shrieking of people as the enemy soldiers caught up with them and attacked. Finally, there would be silence—an absolute, eerie, unnatural silence. No one would be left to make noise. The people would have fled or been killed. This is part of what Zephaniah had in mind when he warned, "The day of the LORD is near" (1:7).

> ¹² **"At that time I will search Jerusalem with lamps**
> **and punish those who are complacent,**
> **who are like wine left on its dregs,**
> **who think, 'The LORD will do nothing,**
> **either good or bad.'**
> ¹³ **Their wealth will be plundered,**
> **their houses demolished.**
> **They will build houses**
> **but not live in them;**
> **they will plant vineyards**
> **but not drink the wine.**

Zephaniah does not want his readers to forget that the real arm of destruction he has been speaking about since verse 10 is not some army of men, some human agent. The real destroyer is the Lord. On the last day, the final "day of the LORD," the Lord will use no agent, other than possibly his angels, to carry out his justice. So here Zephaniah clarifies his picture. Even though he is still describing the activity of an invading army, now it is the Lord himself searching every nook and cranny of the city. The contents of every dark corner will be revealed as the Lord seeks out the wicked, in the manner of invaders searching for soldiers and citizens who have hidden themselves. There is no possibility of hiding from him. Absolutely no one will escape his wrath and punishment.

The objects of the Lord's search are men who are like wine that has been left on its dregs. The dregs are the impurities that settle out of new wine during the fermenting process. The Israelites left that wine on the dregs for a while to strengthen the wine's taste. If the wine was left too long, however, the dregs would embitter the wine, finally turning it into an unusable, jellied mass. The prophet's point is that the wicked in Jerusalem have remained there undisturbed for such a long time that they have grown spiritually smug and complacent. The quality of their spiritual life has been destroyed. They have settled into their wickedness, are beyond redemption, and are totally useless to the Lord. Zephaniah describes their attitude by putting words into their mouths. "The LORD will do nothing, either good or bad," they assert confidently.

These people were not *confessing atheists* who came right out and denied the existence of God. They were *practical atheists*—people who said that his existence didn't matter. In their indifference, they felt that he played no role in their lives. They denied that he was the source of their blessings. They refused to believe that he involved himself with any human affairs, theirs included. They didn't expect him to keep his threats to intervene and punish their wrongdoing. Like spoiled wine, there was nothing left to do with these wicked men but discard them. And what a shock the Lord's judgment would be when it came. The wealth they had spent so much time acquiring would become the spoils of war. The houses they had so proudly built would be razed to the ground. Their marvelously groomed and tended vineyards would become a heap of drying, withering vines. Everything that replaced the Lord in their hearts as a basis for their confidence would be gone. The Lord's judgment on them would rival and surpass any destruction that an invading army can inflict on a defenseless city.

The whole world will be consumed

14 "The great day of the Lord is near—
  near and coming quickly.
 Listen! The cry on the day of the Lord will be bitter,
  the shouting of the warrior there.
15 That day will be a day of wrath,
  a day of distress and anguish,
 a day of trouble and ruin,
  a day of darkness and gloom,
  a day of clouds and blackness,
16 a day of trumpet and battle cry
  against the fortified cities
  and against the corner towers.

Zephaniah ends his chapter by describing the Lord's judgment in a climactic way. After warning that God's day of judgment will strike Judah soon, Zephaniah uses some of the most vivid imagery anywhere in the Bible, to describe what God's final judgment on the earth will be like. His words paint a mural of judgment and wrath that is hard to ignore. In fact, it has not been ignored. The opening line of verse 15, "That day will be a day of wrath," inspired the 13th century Latin hymn *Dies irae, dies illa [Day of Wrath, That Day],* which has been sung in the church ever since on the last Sundays of the church year. It is Hymn 607 in *The Lutheran Hymnal* and appears in *Christian Worship* as Hymn 209. Even in the English translation the hymn manages to capture the unsettling aspect of Zephaniah's words and his subject matter. Fortunately, the hymn as it appears in our hymnbooks also includes the salvation God gives us in Christ which delivers from that day, a topic Zephaniah doesn't treat until chapter 3.

For the second time in this chapter (the first being in verse 8), Zephaniah introduces his theme, the day of the Lord. Here he calls it "the great day of the LORD," to distinguish it from any other preliminary day of judgment which may come on the earth during its history. His chief point, however, is that the day is near. It will be here before anyone expects it. There is little time to prepare. This is the message that the Lord has given throughout the Scriptures through his apostles, his prophets, and his own Son. In fact, the last recorded words of Jesus in the Bible have him saying, "Yes, I am coming soon" (Revelation 22:20).

God says these things so often because his people need to hear them over and over again. We tend not to have the same view of time that the Lord does. Two thousand six hundred years ago, Zephaniah said the day of the Lord was near. And two thousand years have passed since the exalted Christ spoke to the apostle John in Revelation. As you and I mark the passing of days and years, that's a very long time. Without the Lord's constant reminder that the end is coming soon, our spiritual sense would become dull. We would become like the unbelieving scoffers that Peter describes: "They will say, 'Where is this "coming" he promised? Ever since our fathers died, everything goes on as it has since the beginning of creation'" (2 Peter 3:4). With the help of the Lord's Spirit, we confidently say, "The end is just around the corner." For that day is near at *any* moment and *every* moment—in Zephaniah's day, in Jesus' day, in Paul and Peter's day, or in our day.

Do you want to know, Zephaniah asks, how close the day of the Lord is? Listen! It's so close that you can hear it—if you listen with ears that have been instructed by the Word of the Lord. Zephaniah is not describing what he thinks might happen on that day. No, he describes what he sees and hears with the eyes and ears of faith, and his words in the original Hebrew sound the alarm much more strongly than the NIV translation does. We can attempt to reproduce the gist of them in this way: "Listen! Do you hear it? The day of the Lord! Bitterly the warrior is shouting there!" It is unclear whether "warrior" is referring to the Lord or not. A few translations understand it as being the Lord. Then the Lord would be playing the role of the warrior as he invades the city and shouts a bitter message of doom and destruction upon the inhabitants. Most commentators, on the other hand, see the warrior as one of the defenders of the city. As the day of the Lord falls upon the city, the defender on the wall is the first to cry out in anguish at the terrible judgment that is about to come upon him and his fellow citizens. Either way, Zephaniah can hear the horrifying sounds as the day of the Lord begins.

At the beginning of this chapter, Zephaniah suggested that the "day of the LORD" would reverse creation. God would "sweep away everything" that he had created (1:2). Commentators suggest that Zephaniah is saying the same thing in verse 15. God created the world in six days. Here Zephaniah mentions the day of the Lord six times. It will reverse everything God did in those first six days of the earth's history and will bring that history to a close.

> That day (1) will be "a day of wrath." According-
> ing to the prophet Amos (5:18), the Israelites
> thought that the day of the Lord would be
> the day on which the Lord would exalt Israel

at the expense of the other nations of the world and that they would be totally exempt from the punishment and destruction that day would bring. Not so, says Zephaniah. It will be a day on which the Lord punishes sin and wickedness, a day on which he gives full expression to his wrath. Beware!

That day (2) will be "a day of distress and anguish" and (3) "a day of trouble and ruin." Words seem to fail the prophet as he struggles to describe what God permits him to see. To compensate he heaps up all the terms he can find for the suffering and the mental and spiritual despair that will accompany it. The description reminds us of Jesus' words, "There will be weeping and gnashing of teeth" (Matthew 22:13).

That day (4) will be "a day of darkness and gloom," (5) "a day of clouds and blackness." Again the terms are piled up. What a reversal of creation! On the first day of creation God called out in the darkness, "Let there be light," and light, the basic ingredient for life, came into existence. Now God calls out in judgment, "Let there be darkness!" and sinners are separated from the life-giving God, cast into the eternal night. No battlefield or conquered city—with suffocating smoke rising from its burning buildings and the odious stench of death rising from the corpses rotting in its streets—ever presented a more hideous scene than the one Zephaniah paints of the world's end.

That day (6) will be "a day of trumpet and battle cry." The day of the Lord's judgment will be unstoppable. It will roll forward like the mightiest army the world has ever seen. No walls or towers of human construction will be able to prevent it from happening or will protect people from its destructive power.

> [17] **I will bring distress on the people**
>   **and they will walk like blind men,**
>   **because they have sinned against the LORD.**
>   **Their blood will be poured out like dust**
>   **and their entrails like filth.**
> [18] **Neither their silver nor their gold**
>   **will be able to save them**
>   **on the day of the LORD's wrath.**
>   **In the fire of his jealousy**
>   **the whole world will be consumed,**
>   **for he will make a sudden end**
>   **of all who live in the earth."**

Zephaniah now describes the consequences of the day of the Lord. None of them are pleasant to contemplate. The vehicle Zephaniah uses to portray that day continues to be the picture of battle—here the aftermath of the city's destruction. Conquered cities nearly always had survivors, but as Zephaniah describes these survivors, they might well wish they were dead. They walk like blind men, staggering about, groping their way—perhaps because their eyes have been gouged out or perhaps because they're in shock, grieving over the loss of everyone and everything that ever meant anything to them. Some of their fellow citizens are not so fortunate—if we can call any of these survivors' fates "fortunate." These citizens lie on the streets with their blood, their very life, running down the sides of the road. Their entrails (intestines) are scattered in the dust, having spilled out from the gaping wound caused by the sword that disemboweled them and took their life. If we have never seen such a battle scene in our lives, then the picture of an animal struck by a car, lying on the road with its blood and guts scattered about, will have to suffice. The difference here is that Zephaniah's dead are not animals. They are people, whom the Lord intended to be the eternal crown of his creation. The Lord's judgment does not play favorites, either. There is no bribing this judge. Silver or gold won't save anyone. The high-born and low-born alike are lying in the street. They are all equally dead. Rich and poor alike are among the survivors. They are all equally destitute.

As we read Zephaniah's words, we must never forget that he is using images and pictures to make his points. *The pictures* and *the reality* being described by the pictures are not identical. Zephaniah uses the picture of battle and the conquest of a city to illustrate the Lord's final judgment. He probably does so because the fall of Jerusalem to the Babylonians was an instance of the Lord's judgment and was to remind them of the final day. But battles and a day of judgment are not identical. For instance, a battle may leave people in one of two states: they may be dazed survivors, or they may be dead. Judgment day will have only one result. Those who come under the Lord's wrath will be cast into the pit of hell to suffer the agony of eternal death—separated from God, dying, but never annihilated. We are to see the prophet's main point from the illustrations he uses, but we should not press the details.

Zephaniah very clearly sets forth *the reason* for the day of the Lord as well. It comes because people have "sinned against the LORD." What a sober reminder of the true nature of sin. Sin is not something God can easily overlook. It is not a series of minor infractions that really are of no consequence. Sin is a living power that rules in the hearts of people. It is willing rebellion against God and everything he stands for. It calls forth the full heat of his furious anger.

"In the fire of his jealousy the whole world will be consumed." These words of Zephaniah present a picture that sinners do not like to contemplate. Sinners like to think that the Lord is a God who, in love, overlooks sin, whose love is so strong that sin doesn't faze him. The picture of the Lord as a kindly old grandfather who simply can't bring himself to punish his naughty grandkids is a picture sinners can be comfortable with—and they refuse to acknowledge the Lord if he is anything other than that. Such a god, of course, makes Christ unnecessary. The Bible tells us that Christ satisfied God's anger against sin. If God's anger against sin, all sin, was not real, Christ did not have to die, and his resurrection is meaningless. Sinners in their blindness caricature the love of God and grossly underestimate his holiness. That's an eternally fatal mistake.

Zephaniah removes our blindness quickly. He gives us a picture of the holy God in action, a holy God who hates sin. The Lord's jealousy is not some base emotion that controls him. It is the expression of his supreme right to be obeyed by his creatures. When that obedience is not forthcoming, the sinner has only the fiery destruction of God's wrath to look forward to. We don't have to like this portrait of God, we just have to know it's true and cry out for the mercy he wishes to bestow upon us. To do otherwise would be the height of foolishness.

Zephaniah closes this chapter in the same way he began. "Make no mistake what I am talking about," he declares. "The day is coming soon when the Lord will suddenly end the earth's existence. The earth and all who live on it will be consumed. Be prepared!"

2

Gather together, gather together,
    O shameful nation,
² before the appointed time arrives
    and that day sweeps on like chaff,
before the fierce anger of the Lord comes upon you,
    before the day of the Lord's wrath comes upon you.
³ Seek the Lord, all you humble of the land,
    you who do what he commands.
Seek righteousness, seek humility;
    perhaps you will be sheltered
    on the day of the Lord's anger.

The words of the last chapter were frightening! They speak of a disaster headed straight toward Jerusalem and toward a sinful world. They describe the Lord's judgment as though it were a huge asteroid plunging directly toward earth. There's no way it will miss. There's no way for the entire earth to avoid being engulfed in fiery destruction. There's no time to take evasive action.

So what should people do? Should they just shrug their shoulders and wait for the inevitable? That seems like a rather hopeless course of action. Should they at least make an attempt to escape the coming destruction? But how can they? What can they do? Can they find a way to fool the judge who will send down this worldwide judgment or bribe him or at least hide from him? The truth is that his all-seeing eyes peer into the very depths of each individual's heart. He can't be bribed. In his holiness he says that the guilty—and that is all sinners—will be punished. There's no place to hide from him either. The highest mountains and the deepest depths of the ocean are all equally accessible to him. Even the grave is not a place where a person can escape from his wrath. In view of the Lord's revelation of his all-encompassing judgment, the only conclusion any sinner can come to is "There is no escape. There is no hope for me!"

Yet there is a way of escape, but it is not one that people have devised. Rather, it comes from the Lord himself. "Repent," he calls out, "before the terrible day arrives." Remember who is issuing this call. It comes from the Lord who takes no pleasure in the death of the wicked but who wants the wicked to turn from their ways and live. As he would later say through Ezekiel, the Lord calls out through Zephaniah: "Repent and live!" (Ezekiel 18:32).

The call to repentance begins with an invitation. "Gather [yourselves] together," the prophet pleads. The word Zephaniah uses has the thought in it of gathering up straw from the field. The picture is a fitting one. As a person gathers up straw into a sheaf, or bundle, so repentant sinners should gather themselves together before the Lord, pleading for his mercy—and do so before the time comes when he gathers them together for judgment. The stooped-over posture that workers assume to gather straw also serves as a fitting picture for the way a sinner should approach God. Perhaps Zephaniah had both ideas in mind when he used this particular word.

The word that the NIV translates as "shameful" is a difficult word to comprehend fully. It actually comes from the same root as the Hebrew word for "silver." The word seems to imply something pale, without color. With that in mind, the Israelites used it to describe a person drained of color or overcome by a fright-filled sense of shame. The same word was used in Psalm 84:2 with the meaning "to long for." There the psalmist says, "My soul yearns . . . for the courts of the LORD." It's not clear whether Zephaniah had one or all of these thoughts in mind when he addressed the nation of Israel as he did: "O shameful nation."

The sense of his call to repentance could perhaps be paraphrased in this way: "O nation that is shameless about its wickedness and unresponsive to the Lord's call to repentance, bow low before the Lord in humble contrition before it is too late and he crushes you with his judgment." Zephaniah would then be describing Israel in a way that is characteristic of all sinners. By nature the sinner either does not recognize his sin as evil and wrong, or he isn't particularly upset about it. He certainly is not willing to bow before the Lord and confess that he is deserving of eternal punishment. By nature every sinner is unresponsive to the Lord.

Zephaniah follows his call for repentance with three clauses that begin with "before." Each of them contains a reason why Israel should respond positively and quickly. Repent, Zephaniah says, "before the appointed time arrives." On his calendar, the Lord has already marked the date when he will act, and that specific, already designated date is "near and coming quickly" (1:14). Sinners tend to think that if the Lord's judgment is going to come at all, it will come at some distant and remote time in the far-off future. So they figure that there is plenty of time to get ready for it. Zephaniah says that's not the case. The Lord's sense of time is different from ours. His patience may make it look as if he hasn't really determined when judgment day will arrive, but sinners are lulling themselves into a dangerous apathy if they view the Lord's plans in this way. He will catch them unprepared. And when he does, they will be swept to their eternal destruction the way the wind catches chaff and blows it into oblivion.

The second reason Zephaniah gives for immediate repentance is this: the Lord's day will be a day of his "fierce anger." The prophet Amos reveals that the Israelites entertained false ideas about the day of the Lord (5:18). Since the prophets had spoken about the "restoration" of God's people, Israel felt that the day of the Lord would, indeed, be a day of judgment—for all the other nations around them.

But they believed they would escape the judgment because they were God's chosen nation. So the Israelites assumed that they didn't need to repent or live godly lives. Zephaniah, however, assures unrepentant Israel that the Lord's anger will indeed burn against them because of their sin.

Once again, Zephaniah's words are unsettling. We tend to think that God's anger can't possibly be so absolute that it will ignore no sin, that no one will escape unscathed. And we like to comfort ourselves by saying, "Oh yes, those wicked people will get what they deserve. After all, they're much worse than we are. Certainly God will see to it that we receive milder treatment." Zephaniah doesn't see it that way. He makes no such comparisons or exceptions. He says, "Be warned, for the Lord's fierce anger will come upon you. He's no God to trifle with." Yes, the reasons for any and all sinners who hear or read Zephaniah's words to repent as quickly as possible are both strong and compelling.

Again Zephaniah calls for repentance. "Seek the Lord," he advises, speaking now particularly to the "humble of the land." The word Zephaniah uses for "humble" is the same word that means "oppressed." That's a good word to use to describe the humble, godly person who seeks to do what is right. Oppression, you see, is not something we seek out and then willingly place upon ourselves. If it comes at all, *it comes from the outside*—it comes from another person who *inflicts oppression upon us,* and that's the way it is with those who stand humbly before God. Their humility is not an attitude they have created or conjured up in themselves. True humility, or contrition, comes from the heavy hammer of God's law, which crushes sinners and tells them that they don't have a chance of standing before the divine Judge and being declared not guilty. God's holy law beats sinners down until they realize the truth that there's nothing they can do, that there is no righteousness they can perform that will be pleasing to the Lord and turn away his fierce anger.

But to those who have been humbled and oppressed by the Lord's law, Zephaniah offers hope. He tells them to "seek humility" because that turns sinners away from their own solutions for the problem of escaping the Lord's anger. Then he says, "Seek righteousness." That, finally, is the way to stand before God and live—to seek a righteousness that is acceptable to him. But therein lies the problem. What righteousness is acceptable to the Lord? What thoughts, words, or deeds will be proclaimed good and right by the Lord? Isaiah tells us not to expect to produce that righteousness on our own or to find it in ourselves. He says, "All of us have become like one who is unclean, and all our righteous acts are like filthy rags; we all shrivel up like a leaf, and like the wind our sins sweep us away" (Isaiah 64:6). That certainly sounds like a hopeless dead end. Is Zephaniah offering a false hope, one that really does not exist, when he says, "Seek righteousness"?

Saint Paul answers the question we have just asked about Zephaniah. The righteousness we are to seek *is not one which we produce,* but *one which the Lord gives.* Paul says, "A righteousness from God, apart from law, has been made known, to which the Law and the Prophets testify. This righteousness from God comes through faith in Jesus Christ to all who believe. There is no difference, for all have sinned and fall short of the glory of God, and are justified freely by his grace through the redemption that came by Christ Jesus" (Romans 3:21-24). The people of Zephaniah's day were not ignorant of this righteousness even though they lived before the time of Saint Paul. At Zephaniah's time, Isaiah's words—which proclaimed that the Servant of the Lord would not demand what was just and right from his subjects when he came—were already over 75 years old. He, the Messiah, the promised Savior—the Suffering Servant, as Isaiah called him—would supply that righteousness for his subjects. "Here is my servant, whom I uphold, my chosen one in whom I delight; I will put my Spirit on him and he will bring justice to the nations. . . . In faithfulness he will bring forth justice; he will not falter or be discouraged till he establishes justice on earth" (Isaiah 42:1,3,4).

A clue to the fact that Zephaniah has Christ's righteousness in mind lies in the words that follow his call for humility: "perhaps you will be sheltered on the day of the LORD's anger." Centuries earlier, when the Lord was preparing to lead Israel out of Egypt under Moses, he taught his people that there was a way to be sheltered and hidden from his wrath, a way that he himself would provide. Before the final plague came over Egypt and destroyed all of the firstborn, the Lord had Moses institute the Passover. Every household among the Israelites was to kill a lamb and smear its blood on the doorjambs of the house. When the Lord swept through the land of Egypt in his anger, he would see the blood on the houses of the Israelites and pass over them. Because of the blood, they would be sheltered from the Lord's fierce wrath.

The Passover lamb was a type, a shadow or reminder, of Christ. When he came and shed his blood, the place of protection from the anger of God was created for all. John the Baptist pointed to Jesus as he was approaching one day and announced to his disciples, "Look, the Lamb of God, who takes away the sin of the world" (John 1:29). We could rephrase what he said this way: "Behold, the Lamb of God, who shelters us from the fierce anger of God."

The nations will be judged

⁴ Gaza will be abandoned
and Ashkelon left in ruins.
At midday Ashdod will be emptied
and Ekron uprooted.
⁵ Woe to you who live by the sea,
O Kerethite people;
the word of the LORD is against you,
O Canaan, land of the Philistines.

"I will destroy you,
and none will be left."

⁶ The land by the sea, where the Kerethites dwell,
will be a place for shepherds and sheep pens.
⁷ It will belong to the remnant of the house of Judah;
there they will find pasture.
In the evening they will lie down
in the houses of Ashkelon.
The LORD their God will care for them;
he will restore their fortunes.

The section of Zephaniah's book that begins with these verses and runs to the end of the chapter is not unique among the prophets. Many prophets include a section of prophecies that describe God's judgment on surrounding heathen nations. Isaiah (chapters 13–23), Jeremiah (chapters 46–51), Ezekiel (chapters 25–32), and the entire books of Obadiah and Nahum come to mind.

Usually, the nations addressed fall into two categories. The one group includes the nations who lived in the immediate vicinity of Israel—people who competed with the Israelites for the land and resources of the area. Tensions or outright warfare often boiled over between them and Israel. These nations are presented to us as perpetual enemies of the Lord's people Israel and of the Lord himself, under whose protection Israel existed. Such nations would include Tyre in Phoenicia to the northwest; the Aramean states like Damascus and Hamath to the northeast; Ammon, Moab, and Edom to the east and southeast; and Philistia to the southwest.

The other group included nations from farther away—usually the imperialistic nations whose armies often overpowered Israel and made it a vassal state that had to pay tribute or incorporated it as a province of their empires. Assyria and Babylon to the far northeast and east and Egypt to the southwest belonged to this group. They were the superpowers of the ancient Near East. All of these nations were typical of the enemies of the Lord and of his people. At times, God used such powerful enemy nations to discipline or punish his erring people, but eventually, he would rise up in anger against their cruel and haughty ways.

Zephaniah seems to have chosen the nations he included very carefully. There is a definite pattern here. That is not always the case when other prophets speak against the nations. Zephaniah, you will recall, used the first chapter of his book to speak of a worldwide judgment that the Lord would bring upon the earth. In this chapter he uses the familiar prophetic activity of speaking against the nations to make that same point. He chooses nations from each of the four points of the compass. Then, by speaking the Lord's judgment against each of them, he restates and reinforces his point that the Lord is about to judge all of humanity. Right at the center of this group of four lies Israel. The Israelites may be God's people, but if they do not repent, they too will come under the same judgment.

The first direction Zephaniah turns to is the west. There he sees the Philistines who lived along the Mediterranean coast. They were hemmed in by the Mediterranean Sea to the west and the Judean foothills to the east. Their territory was about 10 miles wide at its northern end and about 30 miles wide in the south. The length of Philistia is around 55 miles. Although people called Philistines were living in this area already in the time of Abraham, the very warlike group that gave Samson, Samuel, Saul, and David so much trouble first settled there about 1200 B.C. during the last third of the period of the judges.

The southern tribes of Judah and Benjamin—in Zephaniah's time they made up the kingdom of Judah—were the ones who had the most contact with the Philistines. While the Philistines lived along the Mediterranean coast, the people of Judah and Benjamin lived in the highlands. Between them lay the foothills. Both groups claimed this territory as their own. Samson's struggles with the Philistines and David's battle with the Philistine giant Goliath took place in these western foothills. The relationship between the Israelites and the Philistines might best be described as a perpetual 450-year cold war—smoldering quietly yet dangerously most of the time, and then flaring up periodically into hot, heavy, and intense hate-filled battles. The tides of war swung both ways. Victory or defeat was determined, as are all things, by the Lord. Sometimes he used the Philistines as the rod of his anger to discipline his people. Sometimes he delivered his repentant people Israel from the Philistines. Samson, for example, pretty much fought them to a tie. In Saul's days, however, the Philistines were so dominant that they occupied sections of Benjamin's territory high in the hills. David drove them back into their own territory again and even made them subservient to him. Later—during the time of the divided kingdoms of Israel and Judah—some kings like Uzziah [also called Azariah] had considerable success against them (2 Chronicles 26:6-8). But others had to endure damaging raids (21:16,17). That's the way Israel's war with the Philistines continued on and off throughout the centuries.

Zephaniah addresses the Philistines by mentioning four of the five cities that formed the Philistine confederation: Gaza, Ashkelon, Ashdod, and Ekron. The first three of these were along the coast. Ekron, along with Gath, which is not mentioned, was inland and closer to Judah. Perhaps Zephaniah omits Gath because the constant struggle between Judah and the Philistines to control the city had reduced it to the point where it wasn't worth mentioning in the same breath with the more prosperous cities of the plain. To picture the destruction that the Lord intended to bring upon these Philistine cities—representing, as they did, all the nations to the west of Judah—Zephaniah uses words that sound like the cities involved. "Be abandoned" sounds a little like Gaza in Hebrew. The same can be said about Ekron and the word "uprooted." If Zephaniah had written his prophecy is English, he might have said something like this: "Ekron will be eradicated, and Ashkelon and Ashdod will be turned into piles of ashes."

The name Kerethites, which Zephaniah here uses for the Philistines, is of unknown origin. It is used two other times in the Old Testament, in reference to a nation or tribe (1 Samuel 30:14; Ezekiel 25:16). In both cases it seems to be used, as it is here, as a synonym for the Philistines. During King David's reign the name was also used to designate men who were mercenaries in David's army and who made up the company that served as his most trusted bodyguard (see 2 Samuel 8:18). Many commentators feel that the term has something to do with the original home of the Philistines in the area of Greece and Crete.

At the end of verse 5, Zephaniah speaks to the land in which the Philistines lived. He addresses it, "O Canaan, land of the Philistines." The land where the Philistines lived was part of Canaan. When Joshua led the Israelites into Canaan, segments of the Canaanite society were living there. The Philistines had established a lordship over those earlier inhabitants. But they soon lost their own distinct culture and adopted much of the Canaanite culture—so much so that roughly two centuries after they arrived, they were worshiping Canaanite gods and using Canaanite language. The distinctive pottery they had made when they first came into the land also disappeared from the sites they occupied at this later time. Although the Philistines remained a distinct group in the land until about a generation after Zephaniah's time, in many ways the land of Canaan absorbed the Philistines and changed them. However, in one very noteworthy way the Philistines changed the land. The name Palestine—a derivative of Philistine—is now often used to designate the entire land of Canaan. In a sense, then, the territory is still called the "land of the Philistines."

Regardless of what terms Zephaniah uses to describe the Philistines, we should not lose sight of the real point of Zephaniah's words. "The word of the LORD is against you." "I will destroy you, and none will be left," the Lord says. Shortly after Zephaniah wrote this, many of the Philistines were deported by the same Babylonian armies that conquered Judah. What Zephaniah had prophesied came true: the day of the Lord arrived for Philistia. The Philistine cities were ruined and abandoned, and the populace was uprooted. After that, people of many different cultures lived in their cities. The disappearance of the Philistines is once again a foreshadowing of the Lord's judgment upon the entire world.

The last two verses of this prophecy against the Philistines reminds Zephaniah's readers that the destruction of the Lord's enemies means the deliverance and prosperity of God's people. The prophet pictures the people of Judah as moving their flocks into Philistine territory and taking their rest in Philistine homes. The Philistine lands would become their possession. This could happen only if the Philistines were no longer there to defend their turf. The imagery has a universal application. Just as the life of the Israelites would have been considerably more enjoyable if the Philistine presence had been removed, so the Lord's people will prosper when the Lord, in the destruction of the Last Day, removes all enemies and all wickedness.

Note that the prophet says that a "remnant" of Judah will experience these blessings from the Lord. The people of Judah would not automatically be blessed simply because they were related by blood to the rest of the nation that the Lord chose to be his own. If individuals in that nation did not repent, they, regardless of their bloodline, would suffer the same punishment as the Philistines. Only the humble in Israel, only those who sought the Lord's righteousness, would be so blessed.

The word in verse 6 translated as "Kerethites" by the NIV is a different word from the one in verse 5. It may be a word that means "wells." At least that's how some other translations understand it. If that's the case, then Zephaniah is using another play on words which sound similar, for that word and the word for "Kerethite" look and sound very much alike.

The word that ends verse 7 is also a difficult one. The meaning that the NIV chose to include in the text, "fortunes," is to be preferred over the one relegated to the footnote, "captives."

> [8] **"I have heard the insults of Moab**
> **and the taunts of the Ammonites,**
> **who insulted my people**
> **and made threats against their land.**

⁹ Therefore, as surely as I live,"
    declares the LORD Almighty, the God of Israel,
    "surely Moab will become like Sodom,
        the Ammonites like Gomorrah—
    a place of weeds and salt pits,
        a wasteland forever.
    The remnant of my people will plunder them;
        the survivors of my nation will inherit their land."

¹⁰ This is what they will get in return for their pride,
        for insulting and mocking the people of the LORD
            Almighty.
¹¹ The LORD will be awesome to them
        when he destroys all the gods of the land.
    The nations on every shore will worship him,
        every one in its own land.

Zephaniah now turns around and faces east. There, on the other side of the Jordan, he sees the nations of Moab and Ammon. The Lord's complaint against these two nations is essentially the same. He accuses them of insulting Israel and making threats against Israelite territory.

Moab occupied the territory along the southern half of the Dead Sea's eastern shore, south of the Arnon River. Moab proved to be Israel's enemy already at the time when Moses led Israel to the Transjordan, prior to the time they entered Canaan under Joshua. Moab's King Balak hired a sorcerer named Balaam to curse the Israelites (Numbers 22–24). When that didn't work, Balaam advised the Moabites to tempt Israel to forsake the Lord. He reasoned that while the Lord might not forsake his people, God's people might forsake him and thus call down judgment upon themselves. He was right, and Israel suffered much damage as a result (Numbers 25).

Later, when the land immediately to the north of Moab was given to the tribe of Reuben by Moses, the Moabites claimed it for themselves. Constant and often deadly skirmishes were the result. During the time of the judges, Moab was one of the nations that oppressed Israel (Judges 3:12-14). Kings like David and Ahab conquered Moab, but Moab soon managed to free itself from Israelite control. The warfare between Moab and Israel never seemed to let up. The books of Kings and Chronicles report many bloody conflicts between the two, as they raided or invaded or occupied each other's territory. The Moabites were the descendants of Abraham's nephew Lot, and were therefore related to Israel, but they certainly were not Israel's friends.

The same could be said about the Ammonites. They too were descendants of Lot, and they lived next to Israel in the Transjordan. They lived north of the Moabite territory and were kind of boxed in between the Israelite land in the Transjordan to the west and the inhospitable desert to the east. The city of Rabbah—now called Amman, in the present-day country of Jordan—was their capital. They were always looking for a chance to gain an advantage against Israel and to increase their territory at Israel's expense. During the time of the judge Jephthah, the Ammonites were strong enough to lay claim to the land given to Reuben and Gad. It took the Lord working through Jephthah to drive them off. David fought wars against the Ammonites as well. Like Moab, they were Israel's constant adversaries.

The Lord proclaims that the lands of Moab and Ammon would become like the territory of Sodom and Gomorrah—totally useless and uninhabitable. Archaeologists are not sure where Sodom and Gomorrah were located before the Lord destroyed them. The 13th and 19th chapters of Genesis would seem to place them either south of the Dead Sea or, perhaps, even under what is now the southern portion of that sea. The southern portion of the Dead Sea is less than 20 feet deep, as opposed to the northern part, which is over

1,000 feet deep. So completely did the Lord destroy those cities that no remains of those two doomed cities have ever been found—either in the Dead Sea's shallow southern waters or on its southern shore. All that is left in that area is the desolate, mineral-covered shore of the sea, where absolutely nothing grows. For Zephaniah to liken Moab and Ammon to Sodom and Gomorrah was to proclaim complete destruction and absolute oblivion for these people. Their pride and their insulting animosity toward the people of the Lord deserved nothing less. They become a good model for the complete worldwide destruction that the Lord through Zephaniah has threatened to bring upon the earth.

The final verse of this section provides a surprising conclusion to this prophecy. At the close of the prophecy against the Philistines, the Lord had promised that the believing remnant of Judah would be blessed. Now he says that people from other nations will join this remnant and be blessed as well. It is a theme which he will develop more fully in 3:9-11. The opening words of the verse, "The LORD will be awesome to them," could mean that the destruction the Lord will bring upon them will fill them with such awesome dread of so powerful a God that they will fall down before him even though their hearts are full of hate. But the verses from chapter 3 indicate that just the opposite would be true. The Lord says that he is going to destroy (literally, "starve") "all the gods of the land." What the Lord has in mind is that he will take all the worshipers away from these false gods. The false gods will have no one to feed them with sacrifices, and so they will starve. Meanwhile, these people from Moab and Ammon will join groups of people from the other nations of the world as they bow in true faith and love before the God of heaven and earth, the Lord, who is their Savior too. Zephaniah sees a worldwide destruction, but he also sees a worldwide salvation, with people from every land making up the population of the Lord's eternal house.

¹² "You too, O Cushites,
will be slain by my sword."

While looking west and east, Zephaniah chose nations from the inner circle of Israel's enemies, nations that lived close by. Now as he looks south and then north, he sees enemies from the outer circle, nations that lived far away, more remote enemies of Judah. Both groups still had an adverse effect upon the Lord's people.

Cush was a nation descended from Noah's son Ham (Genesis 10:6). The Cushites lived in the land of Nubia, or ancient Ethiopia (not to be confused with modern Ethiopia, which is farther to the south), which was on the southern border of Egypt, the site of the present-day Aswan dam. Usually, Cush was under the domination of Egypt, but in the century before Zephaniah wrote, the Cushites actually established a dynasty of pharaohs over Egypt. They ruled for roughly 50 years (715–663 B.C.). This may be the reason why Zephaniah picked Cush as his nation from the south instead of Egypt, which would seem to have been the more natural choice.

Cush was not one of the perennial enemies of Israel like most of the countries previously mentioned. The writer of 2 Chronicles reports that some time in the ninth century B.C. a Cushite named Zerah attacked Asa, king of Judah, with a huge army but went down to defeat (14:9-15). Zerah was probably a general in the Egyptian army and so was not representing the Cushite nation as such. Isaiah also includes a section on Cush (18:1-7), but he doesn't prophesy its destruction there. In fact, at the end of the section Isaiah speaks of Cushites coming to worship the Lord. Two chapters later he lumps Cush together with Egypt—probably because of the Cushite dynasty, which would have been in power during Isaiah's ministry—and proclaims that their power will be overthrown. Otherwise, the prophets are silent concerning Cush, and its contacts with Israel were minimal.

The striking thing about this prophecy is not just who is addressed. It also has to be the shortest prophecy by any prophet against any nation. Zephaniah uses just one sentence to prophesy that Cush would be destroyed by the Lord's sword. That sword of which he speaks may belong to Nebuchadnezzar, because it was his army that roamed freely through the lands to the northwest of Egypt and then entered the delta region of the Nile to harass the Egyptians themselves. Perhaps the reason for the brevity of Zephaniah's words is that he wants to leave the impression that Cush is a remote nation about whom little was known. This would help to make Zephaniah's point that *all* nations—yes, even unknown and remote nations—will come under the Lord's judgment. No one will escape Israel's God. No nation is so far away that it is outside his far-reaching threats to punish the wicked when the world ends.

> ¹³ **He will stretch out his hand against the north**
> **and destroy Assyria,**
> **leaving Nineveh utterly desolate**
> **and dry as the desert.**
> ¹⁴ **Flocks and herds will lie down there,**
> **creatures of every kind.**
> **The desert owl and the screech owl**
> **will roost on her columns.**
> **Their calls will echo through the windows,**
> **rubble will be in the doorways,**
> **the beams of cedar will be exposed.**

¹⁵ **This is the carefree city**
    that lived in safety.
She said to herself,
    "I am, and there is none besides me."
What a ruin she has become,
    a lair for wild beasts!
All who pass by her scoff
    and shake their fists.

Finally, Zephaniah turns to the north. He looks past regional enemies like Damascus, even though in earlier years that Aramean city-state had waged many bitter battles against the Israelites. He probably overlooks it because its power had been broken by Assyria some one hundred years earlier, and the city never managed to recover and reclaim its former glory. No, Zephaniah looks some seven hundred miles away to the most powerful and dreaded enemy either Israel or Judah had ever faced—the nation of Assyria.

Here was an aggressive, imperialistic nation that had bothered the Israelites for about two hundred years and had dominated them for the last century. Jehu, king of Israel, paid tribute to the king of Assyria after he usurped the throne of Israel from Ahab's son in 841 B.C. About a century later Tiglath-Pileser III incorporated the northern area of Israel around the Sea of Galilee into the Assyrian Empire as a province. At the same time, Ahaz, king of Judah, was a fawning vassal of Assyria, much to Isaiah's chagrin (see Isaiah 7). Ten years later in 722 B.C. the Assyrian kings Shalmaneser V and Sargon II conquered Samaria and deported the people of Israel to far-off eastern locations in the empire. Then in 701 B.C. the Assyrian king Sennacherib attacked Hezekiah and the city of Jerusalem. It took a miracle from the Lord to prevent the city from falling into his hands. Only a few years beforee Zephaniah spoke, Josiah's grandfather Manasseh had been forced, almost like a prisoner, to make the nine hundred mile trip to Babylon to appear before the Assyrian king and profess his loyalty to the empire. If there ever was a nation that the people of Judah both feared and hated, it was the nation of Assyria.

In pronouncing judgment against Assyria, Zephaniah speaks of the Lord stretching out his hand to the north. Actually, any map of the ancient Near East will show that Assyria is located directly northeast of Canaan. But whenever Assyrian armies invaded Israel, it was always from due north. So Zephaniah chooses Assyria as his nation from the north.

Zephaniah speaks of the destruction of Assyria and its capital city, Nineveh, as something which still lay in the future. This means that Zephaniah must have written these words no later than 612 B.C., the year that Nineveh was destroyed by the Medes and the Babylonians. In fact, he seems to have been writing some 20 years earlier, when the fall of Nineveh was far from a foregone conclusion. His prophecies of Nineveh's fall and destruction must have sounded incredible to his first readers.

What Zephaniah has to say about Nineveh was not unique, however. Nahum's prophecy expresses the same line of thought. Nahum probably was a slightly older contemporary of Zephaniah, and Zephaniah may have been familiar with Nahum's prophecy.

Zephaniah makes two points. He speaks first of all about the total destruction of the city. In Zephaniah's time Nineveh was the grandest city in the world. The city proper together with its suburbs may have had a population of over 600,000 people. It was regarded as the very height of civilization. Its power, wealth, and glory were unmatched in the world at Zephaniah's time. The people of that time would have had a great deal of difficulty imagining how Nineveh could possibly lose the iron grip it held over the nations of the Middle East. Perhaps they could imagine that its power would wane—in the same way that the world influence of London or Moscow has diminished in our day—without totally disappearing. But for the city to disappear from the face of the earth in the way that both Nahum and Zephaniah prophesied would be truly astounding. Yet this is exactly what Zephaniah says would happen. This green and growing city of beautiful parks would become as dry as the desert. This magnificent city inhabited and visited by the most sophisticated people in the world would become a wilderness inhabited only by wild animals and used by lowly shepherds to tend their flocks. The splendid castles and temples that lined Nineveh's streets would be razed to the ground, the costly materials used to beautify their interiors would wind up being exposed to the elements, and the hoots and grunts of roving animals would reverberate and echo off their walls. From top to bottom there would be nothing but ruin and desolation.

Zephaniah also tells us why Nineveh would be the victim of such complete destruction. Such punishment would befall them because of their insufferable arrogance. Zephaniah quotes the city as saying, "I am, and there is none besides me." Compare these words with those the Lord speaks of himself in Isaiah 45:6, "I am the LORD, and there is no other," and you can see what Zephaniah is accusing Nineveh of doing. The city was exalting itself to the level of God himself. Who did this city think it was, putting itself and its plans on the same plane as the Creator of heaven and earth? What wicked pride! The city richly deserved the annihilating punishment it received.

Proud, haughty, and arrogant Nineveh serves as a most fitting representative of the wicked world the Lord has threatened to destroy. After all, every sinful heart and every sinful deed which flows from that heart is an expression of pride and rebellion against the Lord. Such a heart says, "Who is the Lord, that I should obey him? My way is as good as his way, and I owe him no obedience whatsoever. I am accountable to no one but myself."

What arrogance! No wonder the Lord threatens to sweep away the entire world of unbelief and wickedness with one final act of destruction, an act that will obliterate the earth and all its inhabitants as completely as Nineveh was. There is one important difference, however. Nineveh ceased to be the object of the Lord's anger because it ceased to exist. In the final judgment the wicked of this world, from Nineveh and everywhere else, will have to face the Lord's unquenchable anger in hell for an eternity. The prospect of facing such punishment ought to be absolutely terrifying to every sinner.

Zephaniah has looked around Israel from west to east, from south to north. He has looked near and far, and he has consistently seen the same thing. "The great day of the Lord is near. That day will be a day of wrath." The entire world stands under the condemnation of the Lord. He will come, and he will judge—finally, completely, horribly. Let the sinner beware, in Israel, and elsewhere, and repent before it is too late!

Faithless leaders will be condemned

3 Woe to the city of oppressors,
    rebellious and defiled!
² She obeys no one,
    she accepts no correction.
She does not trust in the LORD,
    she does not draw near to her God.
³ Her officials are roaring lions,
    her rulers are evening wolves,
    who leave nothing for the morning.

⁴ **Her prophets are arrogant;**
  they are treacherous men.
Her priests profane the sanctuary
  and do violence to the law.
⁵ **The L**ORD **within her is righteous;**
  he does no wrong.
Morning by morning he dispenses his justice,
  and every new day he does not fail,
  yet the unrighteous know no shame.

These words of Zephaniah echo an earlier situation, one that involved the prophet Nathan. The Lord had sent Nathan to confront King David. David needed confronting. Months earlier he had ruthlessly abused his royal power and privilege and committed adultery with Bathsheba, the wife of Uriah. Then, to cover up his sinful conduct, he planned and set in motion Uriah's murder. Nathan had the task of confronting David with his sin and the Lord's displeasure, but David was in no mood to confess his guilt. How was Nathan to get David to face up to his sin?

Nathan showed himself to be a wise and effective proclaimer of God's Word. He told David a story about a ruthless rich man who killed a poor man's pet lamb—the only one the poor man had—as a meal for his friend rather than using one of the many he himself possessed. As David listened to Nathan's story, he became so angry that he delivered his judgment right there on the spot: "As surely as the LORD lives, the man who did this deserves to die!" (2 Samuel 12:5). That's when Nathan turned to him and said, "You are the man!" (verse 7). David thought he was passing judgment on some else's wickedness. In reality, he was judging himself.

In the opening words of this chapter, Zephaniah acts much like Nathan. He has been condemning Judah's neighbors for their wickedness and has announced that they would be crushed by God's judgment. We can almost see the people of Judah relaxing and feeling more secure as the Lord's pronouncements of judgment moved farther and farther away from them to fall on nations hundreds of miles away. As they listened to Zephaniah's words of condemnation, the people of Judah probably nodded their heads and said to themselves, "Good. It's about time those wicked heathen got what was coming to them." So when Zephaniah began this chapter with the words "Woe to . . . ," they probably thought he was speaking to people like the Philistines, whom he had previously addressed with similar words (2:5). And when he mentioned "the city of oppressors," their thoughts probably turned to Nineveh, the city Zephaniah had just finished condemning for its arrogant aggression. It's at that point—perhaps just as his readers were ready to nod in agreement once again—that Zephaniah gave them his equivalent of "You are the man."

The woe he speaks in this final chapter of his prophecy is not against Philistia. He is confronting the people of Judah. "The city of oppressors" that he describes in such condemnatory terms is not Nineveh or some other foreign capital city. No. "The city of oppressors," Zephaniah says, is Jerusalem. It was this Jerusalem, the city in which the Lord had established his earthly dwelling place, that had sinned. It was Jerusalem that Zephaniah was calling to repentance. It's true that Jerusalem was not the seat of an oppressive, self-seeking world power like Assyria, but the attitude of its heart and the way its leaders treated their own people showed that it really wasn't much different from Assyria and that it deserved a similar condemnation.

What a lesson there is in all this for the people of God! When we hear God condemning the wickedness of unbelievers around us, we too ought to take those words as a call to repentance directed to us, for the same sinful heart dwells in each of us by nature and seeks to express itself in our day-to-day lives. Jesus taught the same truth when he told the Jews of his day, "Why do you look at the speck of sawdust in your brother's eye and pay no attention to the plank in your own eye? . . . First take the plank out of your own eye, and then you will see clearly to remove the speck from your brother's eye" (Matthew 7:3,5).

The prophet had put Judah under the Lord's judgment already in chapter 1. Now he turns his attention back to the Lord's people once again. This time he condemns Jerusalem, using some of the harshest terms any prophet ever used against the city. The word order the NIV uses somewhat softens the fierce blanket condemnation Zephaniah lays on the city. Zephaniah's Hebrew words read this way: "Woe to the rebellious one, the defiled one—the city, the oppressing one." The word Zephaniah uses for "rebellious" is the one that is usually reserved for rebellion against God. *Defilement* speaks of personal, moral pollution in one's life, and *oppression* implies the type of conduct where one person mistreats another for personal gain.

Notice the progression: (1) Jerusalem's leaders were unwilling to submit to the Lord; (2) their lives were defiled by their sins; (3) they abused their neighbors. Without faith in the heart and without a willingness to lead God-pleasing lives, healthy relationships between individuals or in society as a whole are bound to suffer. Society cannot be improved by legislating morality. It can be changed for the better only when the individuals that comprise it are brought out of their sinful rebellion by the gospel of Jesus Christ and, as a result, seek in love to lead their lives according to God's will. Then the mistreatment and abuse of one's neighbor will stop as well.

In verse 2, Zephaniah lays down a fourfold charge against Jerusalem. The first two charges involve unacceptable reactions to the Lord's revealed will. The other two involve fault-worthy responses to his love. Zephaniah says Jerusalem "obeys no one"—especially not the Lord. Instead of recognizing him as the Lord of their lives, the inhabitants of the city were defiant and rebellious and rejected his will for their lives, the way in which he would have them walk. In sinful and rebellious pride they proclaimed, "We have a better way—our way—and no one, not even you, Lord, is going to tell us what to do." Then, when the Lord punished or disciplined them as his erring children, they weren't willing to accept his "correction" either. This too was obvious evidence of their impenitence. It is the unrepentant criminal who complains that the punishment he has been given is unfair. It is the unrepentant child who pouts or screams when his parents discipline him, and it is the unrepentant adult who reacts in anger at the police when he is pulled over or fined for a traffic violation. Such responses of the people of Jerusalem to the Lord's will showed the hardened defiance that lived in their hearts.

Their response to the love of God wasn't any better. Zephaniah says that Jerusalem did "not trust in the Lord." The people had ample evidence of his goodness. Page after page of their history recorded the acts of his deliverance. The land that surrounded them was filled with self-evident proofs of how the Lord had stood by his people, nurtured them, and protected them. But in their unbelief they had considered him to be unworthy of their full-fledged trust. They ignored him because they felt they couldn't count on him. They turned instead to their idols, to their officials, to foreign powers, or to their own abilities. Once such things took the Lord's place in their hearts, they rested their confidence on them and not the Lord. That was an insult to the Lord. It made a statement—an incredibly negative statement. It said that all his goodness meant absolutely nothing.

The result was that they didn't "draw near" to God. Yes, they brought sacrifices and performed other acts of worship. But they did so mechanically and haphazardly, if at all, because their relationship with the Lord was only lukewarm at best. Their prayer life was spotty because they simply weren't willing to lean upon the Lord. They didn't out-and-out deny him, but they were more than willing to go it alone, or at least without him.

Christians often speak of the offices of the Messiah, which Jesus performed while here on earth and continues to do so in heaven. He was our High Priest who both provided the sacrifice of his own body and performed the once-and-for-all sacrifice on the cross. He continues to be our High Priest as he pleads for us, on the basis of his blood, before his Father's throne. Jesus was our Prophet who revealed both the holiness of the Father and his gracious redeeming love for sinners. He still is our Prophet in that he sends his Spirit into our hearts, where, working through the gospel of forgiveness, he creates faith and new life. Jesus was our King who established his reign of grace through his perfect obedience and atoning death—all credited to us before the heavenly Father. He still is our King who through the gospel in Word and sacrament establishes his rule of grace in our hearts and keeps us safe until he takes us to glory.

The earthly representations of these messianic offices were present in Old Testament Israel. The Lord established them for the spiritual blessing and well-being of his people. These offices were to be filled by faithful men who, though not perfect like Christ, would still be fitting shadows of the blessings God had prepared for his people in Christ. In Zephaniah's time, however, just as at other times in Israel's history, the men who held the three highest offices in Israel were utterly failing the people they were called to serve.

Zephaniah says that the *officials* and *rulers,* the king and his royal officials, were no better than roaring lions out to fill their bellies on prey or wolves who greedily gulped down the carrion or prey they had killed until nothing was left. Both animals are used to picture the greed of these rulers—never satisfied, always hungry for new victims, always looking for more gain. Instead of serving the people, these officials used their positions to exploit the people and grow rich at their expense.

The *prophets,* whose responsibility it was to proclaim the Lord's Word and will to the people, were arrogant men caught up in their own importance. To them, receiving the proper honor for who they were and for the position they held was more important than proclaiming God's truth. In addition, the prophets were "treacherous" men in that they really had no regard for the truth but rather proclaimed prophecies which they knew to be false. Rather than being faithful watchmen who warned the people of the consequences of their sins, the prophets preached whatever warm and fuzzy message the people wanted to hear. Their listeners may well have been happy with them and have highly honored them, but their listeners did not hear God's call to repentance from their mouths and lips, nor were their listeners pointed to the God who could and would deliver them.

Finally, the *priests* are called profaners of the sanctuary. The Old Testament priests were the mediators, the go-betweens, between sinful humans and a holy God. Through the blood sacrifices offered by the priests, God was announcing the very heart of his saving truth—that he would accept a substitute for sinners. But by their careless attitudes and negligent performance of their duties, the priests showed that God's holiness and his intense desire to save sinners was no big deal to them. They not only dishonored God with their indifferent service, they also, by their example, led others to do the same.

God also accused the priests of doing "violence to the law," to God's instruction for his people. One of the chief duties of the priests—outside of their work in the temple precincts—was to teach the Law of Moses to the people. But even when they taught the law, they twisted it so as to excuse sinful behavior, thus leaving the impression that God's law held no real claim on *their* lives. Such indifferent and improper teaching of the law of God had the effect of declaring it null and void and blocking it out of the hearts and lives of the people. In short, the priests *were teaching the people how to ignore God,* rather than proclaiming, "Hear, O Israel: The LORD our God, the LORD is one. Love the LORD your God with all your heart and with all your soul and with all your strength" (Deuteronomy 6:4,5).

This sorry picture of the spiritual leaders of Israel ought to have a salutary effect on the Lord's people today. If pastors, teachers, and parents, who are to bring the Word of God to us, are any better than the ones Zephaniah described in this chapter, then it is only because the Lord is faithful and is blessing his people. Faithful leaders who have a servant's attitude toward their work are a blessing of God not to be taken for granted. If we have them, the Lord should be praised and thanked for this blessing. Their work also should be honored and the Lord should be glorified by the way their leadership is followed and their message is accepted.

In glaring contrast to the abominable performance of Judah's kings, prophets, and priests, the Lord stood faithfully at his post. In his "righteousness" he "does no wrong." The Lord's performance for his people will always put the efforts of his people to shame, even when they, in turn, seek to be faithful to him. But here the contrast was so great that the leaders of Israel and those who followed them should have been filled with the greatest shame. Though God's people by their own lack of trust had declared him to be untrustworthy, yet the Lord was there every day, supplying daily bread for body and soul. Though surrounded by evidence that "morning by morning [God] dispenses his justice" and righteousness and wrath and judgment against sinful men and sinful nations, they remained unmoved by all the proof God left them. They continued to lead their lives as if their eyes had not seen God in action and as if their hearts had never felt the Word of God hammering on the door. There was no repentance. The message of true prophets of God, like Zephaniah, fell on deaf ears. "The unrighteous know no shame," Zephaniah said.

> 6 "I have cut off nations;
>> their strongholds are demolished.
> I have left their streets deserted,
>> with no one passing through.
> Their cities are destroyed;
>> no one will be left—no one at all.
> 7 I said to the city,
>> 'Surely you will fear me
>> and accept correction!'
> Then her dwelling would not be cut off,
>> nor all my punishments come upon her.
> But they were still eager
>> to act corruptly in all they did.
> 8 Therefore wait for me," declares the LORD,
>> "for the day I will stand up to testify.
> I have decided to assemble the nations,
>> to gather the kingdoms

and to pour out my wrath on them—
all my fierce anger.
The whole world will be consumed
by the fire of my jealous anger.

A better translation of the beginning of verse 6 might read, "I am determined to cut off nations." The Lord is describing the course of action he is planning on following with the nation of Judah and with the wicked, unbelieving nations of the earth as well. He will cut them off, that is, destroy them completely. Both the "strongholds," the places of refuge, and the people who seek shelter in them will be totally "demolished." The "streets" of the cities of the earth will be "deserted, with no one passing through" them, because the people are all dead. "No one will be left—no one at all." This activity of the Lord, which has been going on throughout history, will reach its climax at the end of the world.

In addition to announcing God's judgment on godless nations, Zephaniah's prophecy was also meant to be a call to repentance for Judah and Jerusalem. The calamities and disasters, natural or man-made, that take place in the world all contain lessons. They are always calls to repentance for God's people. Jesus told his disciples as much when he commented upon the news of a tragic massacre of some Galileans: "Do you think that these Galileans were worse sinners than all the other Galileans because they suffered this way? I tell you, no! But unless you repent, you too will all perish. Or those eighteen who died when the tower in Siloam fell on them—do you think they were more guilty than all the others living in Jerusalem? I tell you, no! But unless you repent, you too will all perish" (Luke 13:2-5).

The Lord's message to Jerusalem about the judgment he had sent and would send upon the cities of the world was

"Surely now that you have seen the fate that befell these other nations, you will fear me and accept correction. Surely now in a spirit of repentance you will stand in awe of my Holy Word and change your life to conform to my will." The Lord eagerly looks for such repentance. He expressed his great willingness to spare Jerusalem and its chosen people from the destruction in store for all the heathen. "Then her dwelling would not be cut off, nor all my punishments come upon her."

What a disappointment, then, for Zephaniah to have to say, "But they were still eager to act corruptly in all they did." Zephaniah observed that the people of Judah and Jerusalem were not only indifferent to the Lord's will, they were "eager" to break it, "to act corruptly in all they did." They couldn't wait to get on with their self-centered lives and their abuse of their neighbors. They persisted in deliberately doing what was wrong, in doing *what they knew* to be wrong. What a sad picture is painted here. Here is the Creator—the Lord of the universe, the One who deserves to be sought out by his creatures—eagerly seeking a relationship with Jerusalem, waiting for his people to respond favorably to his warnings and his love. But what happens? His people ignore him. They rebuff his efforts to come close to them. They reject his invitation to be his people forever.

The Lord warns his people that the day will come when his efforts to win them back will end. The Last Day—which was meant to be a day of destruction for the wicked but a day of deliverance for God's chosen nation—will be a day of destruction for them as well. "Therefore wait for me," the Lord declares. Usually that phrase, "wait for the Lord," is one filled with promise and hope. It usually describes someone who in patient faith is waiting for the Lord to fulfill his promises of deliverance. Using the same word that Zephaniah uses, Isaiah says, "I will wait for the LORD, who is hiding his face from the house of Jacob. I will put my trust in him" (Isaiah 8:17). In Zephaniah's prophecy to unrepentant Judah, however, that phrase has a cruel twist to it. Now it has more the sense of "Just you wait for me. When I come, you'll be sorry."

The Lord now returns to the theme with which Zephaniah began: the Lord will judge the entire earth. This sinful, rebellious world will feel the fiery heat of his anger and be consumed. Worst of all, unrepentant Judah will be caught up in the blaze. Why? While they were in the world, they lived their lives in such a way that they were no different from the unbelievers in the world. And so at the final great "day of the LORD," no distinction will be made between the way they and the rest of the world are to be treated. What a warning to God's people today! The message is clear. Act like the unbelieving world, join the unbelieving world in its impenitent attitude and its godless behavior, and on judgment day you can expect to be treated like the unbelieving world. May the Lord grant us his Holy Spirit through the Word of Christ, to ensure that we escape such a fate.

PART THREE

The Lord's Day Is a Day of Deliverance and Rejoicing
(3:9-20)

The Lord will purify the nation

> ⁹ "Then will I purify the lips of the peoples,
>> that all of them may call on the name of the LORD
>> and serve him shoulder to shoulder.
> ¹⁰ From beyond the rivers of Cush
>> my worshipers, my scattered people,
>> will bring me offerings.
> ¹¹ On that day you will not be put to shame
>> for all the wrongs you have done to me,
> because I will remove from this city
>> those who rejoice in their pride.
> Never again will you be haughty
>> on my holy hill.
> ¹² But I will leave within you
>> the meek and humble,
>> who trust in the name of the LORD.
> ¹³ The remnant of Israel will do no wrong;
>> they will speak no lies,
>> nor will deceit be found in their mouths.
> They will eat and lie down
>> and no one will make them afraid."

Through two and a half chapters of his prophecy, Zephaniah's message has been a harsh one, hard on the ears. God's judgment will be universal. Is Zephaniah, then, a totally law-oriented book? The last dozen verses of Zephaniah's prophecy emphasize that the message of judgment, the message of God's law, is not God's final word to the human race. God's deliverance, his restoration, will be just as universal as his judgment.

Zephaniah uses words in a rather unusual manner in this section. By doing so, he gets our attention and manages to make what he is saying memorable. He has just quoted the Lord as saying, "Wait for me," an expression usually associated with hope and confidence in the Lord's goodness, but as he used the expression here, it meant "Just wait until I get my hands on you." Now in the opening words of this section, the Lord literally says, "I will overturn"—a phrase usually associated with judgment. The book of Genesis, for example, speaks of the Lord "overturning" Sodom and Gomorrah in flames. Here, however, he says, "I will overturn to the peoples a pure speech." In other words, "I will change their hearts so that they confess me rather than curse me."

There are two ways in which the Lord can purify his people. He can declare them not guilty of sin for Christ's sake, and through that marvelous message he can work new life in the hearts of the believers, who then seek to honor and glorify him by obedient living. This is what the Lord promised through Ezekiel: "I will sprinkle clean water on you, and you will be clean; I will cleanse you from all your impurities and from all your idols. I will give you a new heart and put a new spirit in you; I will remove from you your heart of stone and give you a heart of flesh. And I will put my Spirit in you and move you to follow my decrees and be careful to keep my laws" (36:25-27). The Lord is speaking of this first way of purifying the people when he says, "Then will I purify the lips of the peoples."

The second way of purifying the people is through judgment, that is, by removing the wicked and destroying the unbelievers so that all that is left is the believing remnant. That is what the Lord is speaking about in verse 11 where he declares, "I will remove from this city those who rejoice in their pride."

The Lord's work of conversion truly is a miracle worked through his Spirit, and the consequences are amazing. Because of the work that he does in the hearts of the people, the Lord says that lips which formerly had cursed him would now call upon him in faith. People who had ignored the will of God for their lives or willfully resisted any attempt of God's law to call them to repentance would now willingly join with other believers and serve the Lord with one accord. Those who formerly sought only to live for themselves and their own advantage would now seek to glorify the Lord and serve their neighbor. What a transformation the Word of God works in the sinful heart of man!

To "call upon the name of the Lord" can refer to a number of things. It may involve praying to him. It may include praising the Lord in public or private worship. Since the Lord himself called upon his own name before Moses in Exodus 34:5, it must also mean to proclaim his name and all his glorious acts in the company of believers and throughout the world. Regardless of what is all involved, calling upon the name of the Lord is an act of faith, a confession of trust in the Lord for salvation. Therefore, as the prophet Joel declares, "Everyone who calls on the name of the LORD will be saved" (2:32).

The Lord speaks of bringing his scattered believers together from "beyond the rivers of Cush," the country immediately to the south of Egypt. The Lord speaks of the *rivers* of Cush because in that territory the two tributaries of the Nile, the White Nile and the Blue Nile, join to form the Nile River. For the Israelites, Cush was on the southern limits of the known world. So for the Lord to speak as he does here is virtually the same as him saying that he will bring his believers together from the ends of the world.

The "scattered people" of the Lord referred to here could simply be the Jews, who at various times had been scattered throughout the world in exile. But in the Scriptures the term "scattered" is also used to refer to the Gentiles. Isaiah speaks not only of Israel returning to the Lord but also of people from all nations scattered throughout the world coming to the Lord. He says, "Nations will come to your light, and kings to the brightness of your dawn" (Isaiah 60:3). Finally, "my scattered people" has to involve all of the elect of God throughout the world. God will gather his chosen people together in one body, the holy Christian church. There they will call upon the name of the Lord, serve him with their fellow Christians, and place acceptable offerings before his throne of grace.

The Lord says, "You will not be put to shame." Here he is addressing the city of Jerusalem as a whole. The believers should have been embarrassed and ashamed of the wicked people who were a part of the city. The Lord's remedy for this intolerable situation is to *remove* the wicked from the city's midst so that only the "meek and humble" are left. Instead of being filled with the proud and rebellious and self-righteous, Jerusalem will be the dwelling place of those who live in the spirit of repentance and faith and "who trust in the name of the Lord." Their lips will not lie, their mouths will not speak deceiving words, and they will do no wrong in their lives.

These are pretty lofty things to say about the purified city of Jerusalem. When will they happen? To a degree, they already have. Wherever the Spirit of God is present with the life-giving gospel in the midst of his people, there new hearts are created—new hearts which cling in faith to the Savior and live as the Lord describes in these verses. That place is not a physical location, like Jerusalem in the land of Palestine. Rather, it's the holy Christian church on earth, where the Spirit of Christ is present with the means of grace. The perfection described in these words, however, will not be reached on this earth. (See Jesus' parables of the weeds, Matthew 13:24-30, and the net, verses 47-52.) Perfection finally will come on judgment day when the Lord removes all the impure and all the hypocrites from his church and takes it to be with himself in everlasting glory.

The Lord will dwell with his forgiven people

> ¹⁴ **Sing, O Daughter of Zion;**
> **shout aloud, O Israel!**
> **Be glad and rejoice with all your heart,**
> **O Daughter of Jerusalem!**
> ¹⁵ **The LORD has taken away your punishment,**
> **he has turned back your enemy.**
> **The LORD, the King of Israel, is with you;**
> **never again will you fear any harm.**
> ¹⁶ **On that day they will say to Jerusalem,**
> **"Do not fear, O Zion;**
> **do not let your hands hang limp.**
> ¹⁷ **The LORD your God is with you,**
> **he is mighty to save.**
> **He will take great delight in you,**
> **he will quiet you with his love,**
> **he will rejoice over you with singing."**

The prophet interrupts the Lord's words here by breaking into a song of praise, and he calls for the people of God to join him in praising the Lord. He says their hearts should be filled with joy and gladness and their mouths should overflow with praise. The reason is simple and yet compelling: "The LORD has taken away your punishment, he has turned back your enemy." Scripture tells us, "The wages of sin is death" (Romans 6:23) and "The soul who sins is the one who will die" (Ezekiel 18:4). If punishment is gone, and if that great enemy, death, has been removed and what remains of it is simply a sleep of the body until the resurrection, then sin and the guilt associated with it before God must be gone as well.

This is exactly what has happened. Isaiah speaks of the work of the Suffering Servant in these words: "He was pierced for our transgressions, he was crushed for our iniquities; the punishment that brought us peace was upon him, and by his wounds we are healed" (53:5). The punishment our sin deserves has been placed on Christ. Regarding the new covenant that God would establish in Christ, the Lord asserts through Jeremiah, "I will forgive their wickedness and will remember their sins no more" (31:34). Zephaniah can speak the way he does in verse 15 because the Lord in his mercy has taken away the sins of the world. They are removed in Christ, and the terrible consequences of sin have been removed as well. Death and hell are no longer a threat to the one who clings to Christ in faith. Those enemies have been removed forever.

The second consequence of the removal of sin is that God is present in the midst of his people with his protecting power. Isaiah tells us, "Your iniquities have separated you from your God; your sins have hidden his face from you, so that he will not hear" (59:2). The holy God hates sin, and he will not dwell among a sinful people. That's why Isaiah speaks as he does. But when sin is forgiven and its guilt has been removed by Christ, there is no reason why the Lord must stay separated from his people any longer. So Zepha-

niah assures his readers, "The LORD, the King of Israel, is
with you."

Yes, he is with them, protecting them from harm, delivering them from evil, quieting and comforting them in their
fears and anxieties, and empowering their limp hands to
move in service to him. Believe it or not, he actually rejoices
with songs on his lips because they are living in his presence. What a glorious revelation of our God! We are the ones
who should be filled with joy and singing, because we have
the privilege in Christ of living with our God for eternity. But
also note that Zephaniah says that the Lord is just as happy
as we are. He is happy because the goal of his work of
redemption—saving his elect—has been reached. He is joyful
because the purpose of creation—that the crown of creation,
mankind, might live in his presence forever—has been real-
ized. God's universal restoration, purification (3:9), and deliverance from all enemies (verses 15-17) will be an occasion of
joy for God and for his people.

The Lord will restore his people

¹⁸ "The sorrows for the appointed feasts
    I will remove from you;
    they are a burden and a reproach to you.
¹⁹ At that time I will deal
    with all who oppressed you;
I will rescue the lame
    and gather those who have been scattered.
I will give them praise and honor
    in every land where they were put to shame.
²⁰ At that time I will gather you;
    at that time I will bring you home.
I will give you honor and praise
    among all the peoples of the earth
when I restore your fortunes
    before your very eyes,"

                                    says the LORD.

Verse 18 is not easy to translate or understand. Some understand Zephaniah as saying that the Lord will remove those who thought that the appointed festivals of the Israelite church year were an imposition. Some Old Testament worshipers went through the motions of worshiping the Lord in sacrifice and song, but their hearts were not in their worship, and they considered such things an imposition on their lives. God would remove these people from the company of believers.

Others are of the opinion that here the Lord is speaking of the consequences of Babylonian oppression. The Babylonians did not allow God's people to worship and celebrate their appointed feasts and festivals, like the Passover and the Day of Atonement, as they wished. The sense then would be that when God finally restores his people, they will be able to resume worshiping the Lord without any fear of reprisal. Regardless of the way these words are understood, their meaning in the context is clear. The Lord will remove from his people anything that oppresses them. He promises, "At that time I will deal with all who oppressed you." This is true whether those people are the indifferent and the wicked in the midst of God's people or whether they come from the outside.

With a series of pictures, the Lord promises that he will restore his faithful people to a position of honor and praise. No longer will they be a despised and ridiculed minority in a world of unbelief and godless rebellion. The last, great day of the Lord will be a day of universal deliverance. God's people will be the center and joy of God's creation, as he always intended the crown of his creation to be. The Lord's redemption of his own will result in reestablishing the intended order and original beauty of his creation.

What a positive way for Zephaniah to end his book. He began with warnings of worldwide judgment and destruction. With such a message there would seem to be no hope. Such is not the case, however, with the gracious Lord in charge. He changes a situation full of hopelessness and despair into the promise of rescue and restoration and joy. What changes the situation is the grace of God. In indescribable love God took the sin that separated us from him and condemned us to everlasting punishment and instead placed it upon his one and only Son. The result? You and I are heirs of all the promises that close Zephaniah's book—purification, deliverance, and a happy homecoming.

> Hallelujah!
> For our Lord God Almighty reigns.
> Let us rejoice and be glad
> and give him glory! (Revelation 19:6,7)